# SECRET
## WICHITA

*A Guide to the Weird, Wonderful, and Obscure*

Vanessa Whiteside

REEDY PRESS

Copyright © 2023, Reedy Press, LLC
All rights reserved.
Reedy Press
PO Box 5131
St. Louis, MO 63139
www.reedypress.com

No part of this publication may be reproduced or transmitted in any form or by any means, electronic or mechanical, including photocopy, recording, or any information storage and retrieval system, without permission in writing from the publisher. Permissions may be sought directly from Reedy Press at the above mailing address or via our website at www.reedypress.com.

Library of Congress Control Number: 2023938771

ISBN: 9781681064932

Design by Jill Halpin

Unless otherwise indicated, all photos are courtesy of the author or in the public domain.

We (the publisher and the author) have done our best to provide the most accurate information available when this book was completed. However, we make no warranty, guarantee, or promise about the accuracy, completeness, or currency of the information provided, and we expressly disclaim all warranties, express or implied. Please note that attractions, company names, addresses, websites, and phone numbers are subject to change or closure, and this is outside of our control. We are not responsible for any loss, damage, injury, or inconvenience that may occur due to the use of this book. When exploring new destinations, please do your homework before you go. You are responsible for your own safety and health when using this book.

Printed in the United States of America
23 24 25 26 27   5 4 3 2 1

# DEDICATION

For my teachers, who encouraged my love of writing.

# CONTENTS

| | |
|---|---|
| 1 | Acknowledgments |
| 3 | Introduction |
| 4 | Below-Ground Goblin |
| 6 | Isle of Interest |
| 8 | Traditions Reign Supreme |
| 10 | City Founder |
| 12 | Steel Sculpture |
| 14 | Rowdy Route |
| 16 | Ever the Eccentric |
| 18 | Preserved Plane |
| 20 | Mood Flags |
| 22 | Tree Tunnel |
| 24 | Station Sign |
| 26 | Gas Station Grub |
| 28 | Saved By the Bell |
| 30 | Whistle-Stop Wonder |
| 32 | Stellar Stone |
| 34 | Sci-Fi Sculpture |
| 36 | Go Glazy |
| 38 | Path Forward |
| 40 | Fit for Royalty |
| 42 | Colorful Creation |
| 44 | Significant Sign |
| 46 | Ornate Office |
| 48 | Designed to Shine |
| 50 | Lady Liberty |
| 52 | Better in Bronze |
| 54 | Magnificent Murals |
| 56 | The Original Buffalo Bill |
| 58 | Totally Tiki |

| | |
|---|---|
| 60 | Strumming Steel |
| 62 | Frontline Fighters |
| 64 | Home on the Range |
| 66 | Tiny Towns |
| 68 | Movie Legend |
| 70 | Daring Design |
| 72 | Confidential Cocktails |
| 74 | Made in Wichita |
| 76 | Alley Art |
| 78 | Grain Elevator Gallery |
| 80 | Madwoman Makes Mischief |
| 82 | Merry-Go-Round Memories |
| 84 | Spirits Among Us |
| 86 | Baseball Brilliance |
| 88 | Somewhere Over the Rainbow |
| 90 | Twisted Tree Limbs |
| 92 | Moment in Time |
| 94 | Tirelessly Standing |
| 96 | Coffin Curiosity |
| 98 | Bird Characters |
| 100 | Gnome Sweet Gnome |
| 102 | Keen on History |
| 104 | Peaceful Plaza |
| 106 | The Sky's the Limit |
| 108 | Standing Proudly |
| 110 | Warbird Wonder |
| 112 | A Sew-phisticated Place |
| 114 | Small Screen |
| 116 | Back Alley Artwork |
| 118 | Firehouse Food |
| 120 | Antique Artillery |
| 122 | Creative Complex |
| 124 | Work of Art |
| 126 | Colorful Craftsmanship |
| 128 | From the Ashes |

| Page | Title |
|---|---|
| 130 | Open-Faced Fun |
| 132 | Perfected Pizza |
| 134 | Gas Lamp Gridiron |
| 136 | Rainbow Residences |
| 138 | IPA in an Igloo |
| 140 | Historic Hideaway |
| 142 | Monument Masterpiece |
| 144 | Tucked-Away Park |
| 146 | Stone Structure |
| 148 | Animal Art |
| 150 | City's Largest Cigar |
| 152 | Victorious Voyage |
| 154 | Beyond the Books |
| 156 | Play Ball |
| 158 | Keep on Rockin' |
| 160 | Celestial Creation |
| 162 | Sailing Symbol |
| 164 | Fragrant Factory |
| 166 | No Shipping Fees |
| 168 | Under, Over |
| 171 | Sources |
| 180 | Index |

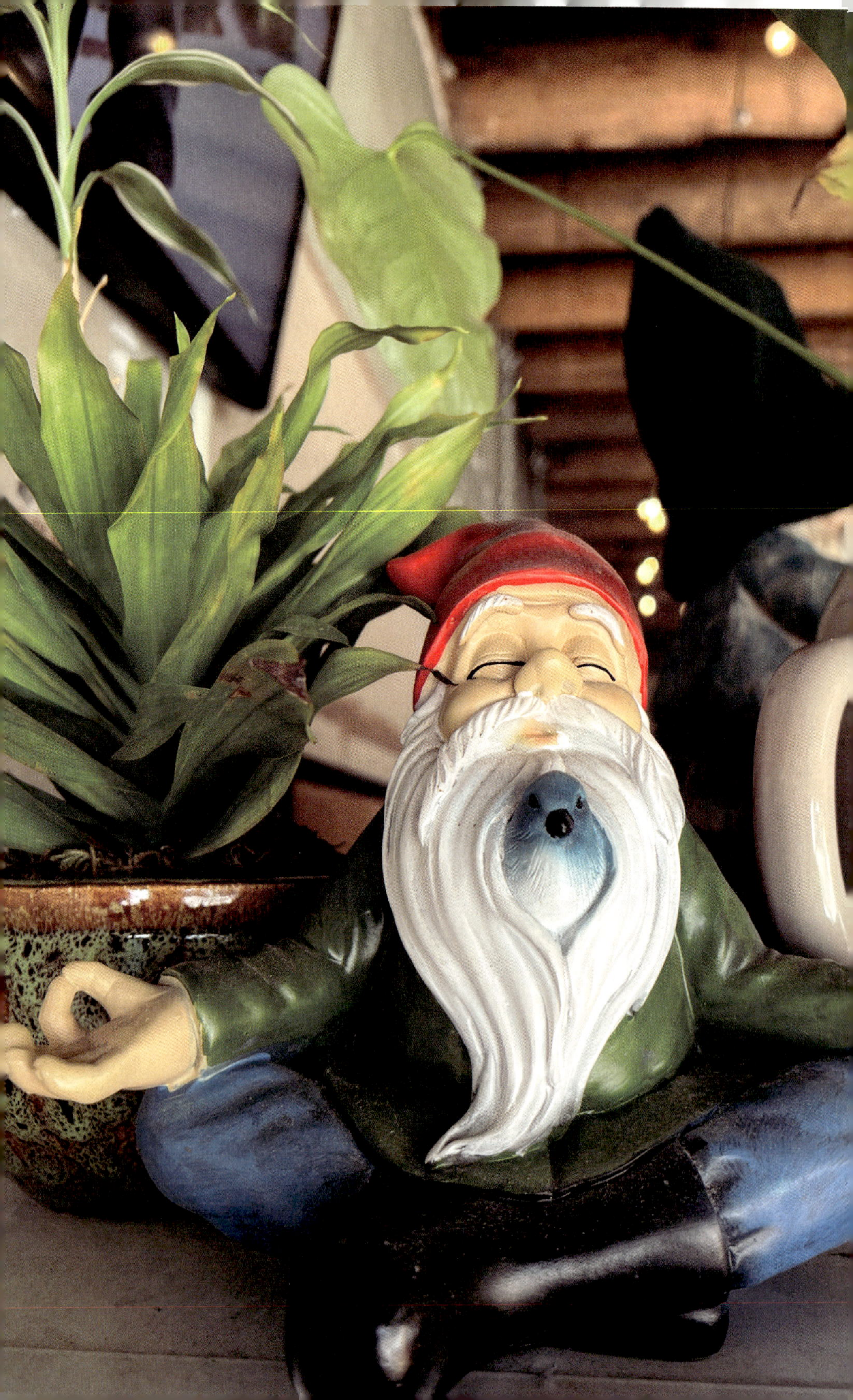

# ACKNOWLEDGMENTS

Often, when people imagine a writer at work, they conjure up an image of a person at a computer, feverishly typing with a constant flow of ideas. In fact, writing a book involves the author leaving the desk to talk with others while conducting research and visiting libraries to thumb through publications. And let's not forget the hours of research done via newspapers.com. Long live print journalism.

I went to the experts to learn more. Several Wichitans volunteered their time answering my questions and collecting information for me. Like the North High School principal, who stopped her no-student work day to give me a tour of the building's tower. Or the restaurant owner who invited me to sit down and listen to how he went about curating antiques. And I would be remiss if I didn't acknowledge the museum employees who contributed directly to this book by digging up information or providing a behind-the-scenes look at exhibits.

Equally important, I'm grateful for family and friends who listened to me talk endlessly about the book. They heard me say, "You won't believe what I learned about Wichita today," and then ask last-minute questions like, "What interesting place am I forgetting?" They shared ideas. They proofread pages. They were some of the first readers to buy a copy of the book.

Of course, I'm appreciative to the Reedy Press team for asking me to write another book and supporting me during the process. From editing the book to securing sales, each employee worked beyond measure to make it possible.

Lastly, and perhaps most importantly, I'm most thankful to you. Of all the books you could have purchased, you chose mine. Like me, you are a curious soul. Someone who likes to ask questions when they see something intriguing. The kind of person who appreciates history.

Writing a book is a monumental task. One day, you glance at the clock and realize you have spent hours researching documents. The next day you are typing excitedly, only to be halted by writer's block. And shooting photos for a book is an undertaking. I must have taken hundreds of images. Ultimately, it was worth it because it allows you to get to know Wichita better.

As I like to remind others, stay curious. It makes life interesting.

# INTRODUCTION

It's interesting how much one can learn about a place if one looks closer.

Does a city have secrets? And what are the stories of its people? I was inspired to write *Secret Wichita: A Guide to the Weird, Wonderful, and Obscure* because I wanted to learn as much as possible about the city's hidden gems, forgotten stories, and intriguing spaces. I let my curiosity take over in pursuit of answers.

As you read this book, you may ask yourself why I chose some of the entries for it. Perhaps what I included isn't necessarily what someone would consider "secret" information, but it most likely creates a sense of wonder. Other places were chosen because they were hidden from view, giving them an obscure quality. And some mentions in the book were added simply because they were downright peculiar, miniature, gigantic, or out of the ordinary. In the end, all of the entries fit one or all of these qualities.

Whether you're a resident of or visitor to the city, I hope *Secret Wichita* ignites your curiosity and encourages you to take a closer look at the city. Use it as a guidebook, checking off places listed in the table of contents one by one. Or perhaps you would prefer to flip its pages, allowing your finger to land on a random page. Enjoy the adventure.

# BELOW-GROUND GOBLIN

**Can you locate the elusive troll hiding underground?**

What lives underground in the city? Some locals don't know a troll lurks underground, spying on passersby as they walk near the Arkansas River in downtown Wichita. It peers through a metal grate from beneath the sidewalk, gazing up at everyone near it. Located near *Keeper of the Plains*, one of the most iconic attractions in the city, is the infamous troll. The public art was installed in May 2007. If you visit it during the day, you can see the goblin clearly. At night, a green light illuminates the sculpture, making it easier to spot the angry-looking monster.

### THE TROLL

**WHAT:** Sculpture

**WHERE:** Under the sidewalk near the bank of the Arkansas River and east of *Keeper of the Plains*.

**COST:** Free

**PRO TIP:** Park in a free public lot at Wichita Veterans Memorial Park and walk to the troll's den using Google Maps as the guide.

Why did the city approve the art installation? It is reported that a design team was challenged by what to do with a concrete storm sewer on the east bank of the Arkansas River. The solution? They designed the space to resemble a troll's cave. Local artist Connie Ernatt, a sculptor and collector, created the troll and is the co-owner of Wichita's gallery, Diver Studio.

Trolls are a symbol of Scandinavian folklore, inhabiting caves or living within isolated rocky areas. Is it a myth or fact? We may never know. To find it, search "Wichita's Troll" to locate the goblin using Google Maps. Walk the sidewalk path toward the river and look down at the sidewalk until you see a metal grate.

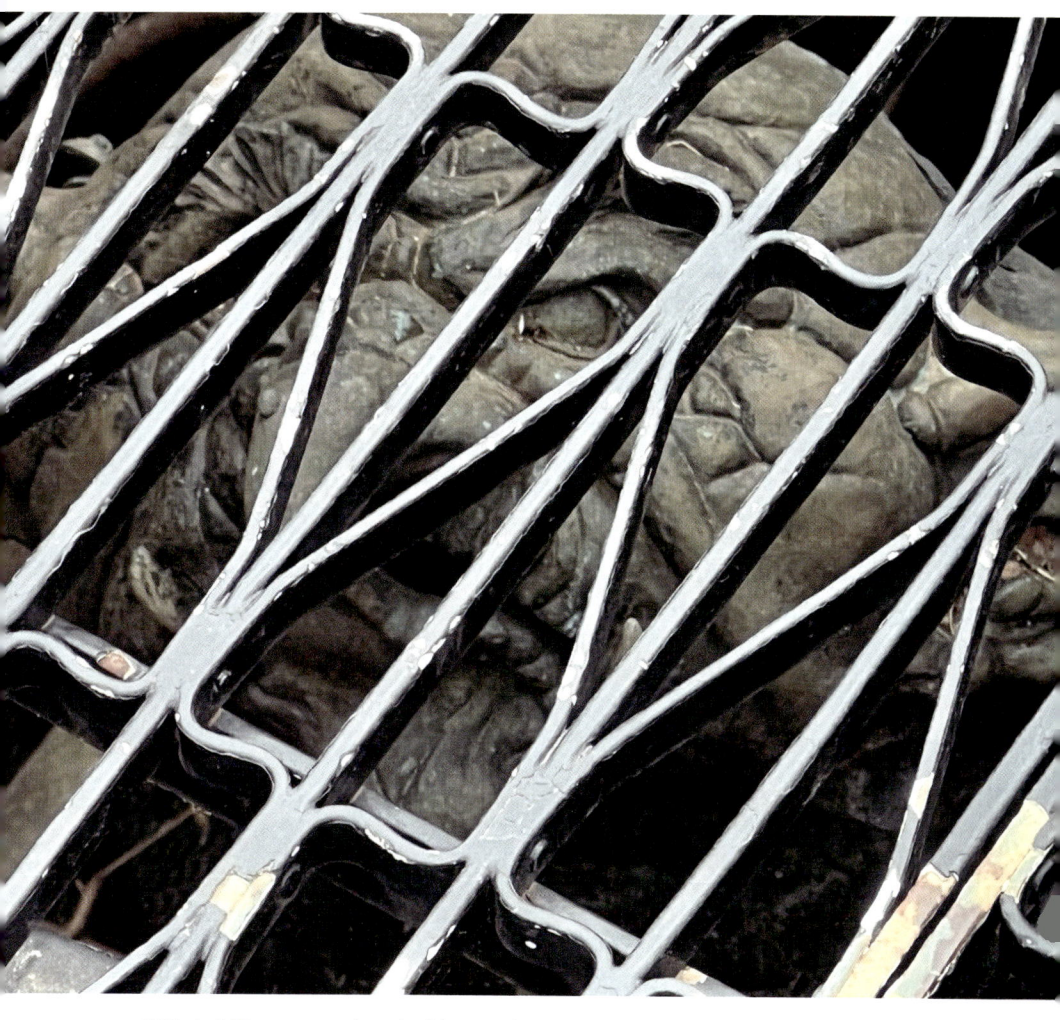

With bat-like ears and a mischievous face, the troll stares back at visitors from its home under the sidewalk in a storm drain.

---

Zerbe Family *Sleeping Troll Hill* at Botanica is another place to view a troll in the city. The massive artwork includes an Astroturf hill, making it possible for kids to roll down the troll's backside.

# ISLE OF INTEREST

**Is it true there was a roller coaster on an island in the middle of the Arkansas River?**

The river in downtown Wichita once looked quite different. By 1886, a sandbar began to resemble an island as the water level of the Arkansas River dropped. Eventually, warranty deeds for the land were transferred to Joseph Ackerman in 1887, and the humble island became known as Ackerman Island. In 1906, it became the home of Wonderland Park, complete with a figure-eight roller coaster. Mayor Finlay Ross said, "The park will be a great thing for Wichita. There will always be someplace to go and be entertained, where you hear good music and see good shows any time." Admission to the park was 25 cents.

The mayor was right. Citizens flocked to Ackerman Island to listen to orchestras and dance, especially on Picnic Sunday. People delighted in using the park's 1,100-seat theatre, skating rink, penny arcade, and billiard hall. In its first year, over 200,000 people visited the island. Years later, the Giant Thriller roller coaster was built when it was decided a bigger and better roller coaster was needed. It was the largest in the country in 1911. The park also was known to host outdoor wrestling and heavyweight boxing matches. Its baseball stadium, Island Park, drew a crowd.

Wonderland Park closed in 1918. The wooden ballpark burned down, likely because of a discarded cigarette, and soon after, the baseball team packed up and left town. Blue laws did not allow business to be conducted on Sundays, causing Wonderland Park to lose money. Plus, the popularity of the automobile increased.

---

After Wonderful Park closed, Ackerman Island was vandalized and in bad shape until Arkansas Valley Interurban occupied the island in 1920 and stayed until the Great Depression.

*The land that occupied some of Ackerman Island is visible in this photo. Wonderland Park was located north of the Douglas Avenue Bridge, in approximately the same area as Exploration Place today.*

## ACKERMAN ISLAND

**WHAT:** Amusement park

**WHERE:** Arkansas River north of Douglas Avenue Bridge

**COST:** Free

**PRO TIP:** View a teaser for the film, *For Your Amusement: The Wonderland Park on Ackerman Island* by Wichitan Sara Joy Harmon, via the film's Facebook page.

Thanks to flooding, Ackerman Island no longer resembled an island, and the ballpark became buried in sand. In 1933, 1,800 men worked to remove the last pieces of the ballpark stands. They hauled wheelbarrows of dirt from the east side and dumped them on the west side of the river to alleviate constant flooding.

# TRADITIONS REIGN SUPREME

**What if the school principal said it was okay to write on the walls?**

North High School, the second-oldest in the city, opened in 1929 to welcome 800 students at the corner of 13th and Rochester streets. Its architecture remains awe-inspiring for its Native American motifs and ascending tower. Built on land settled by Wichita Indians in the 1860s, the school's facade showcases art deco details and references to the land, the river, and the area's early residents. But it's the builder's tower that garners the most attention and is central to the school's traditions. Since the 1930s, graduating seniors are granted permission to scale the tower's spiral staircase and write on its interior walls. Parting messages include phrases like, "I can see my house from here," "I did it," and "See ya!", written in black Sharpie®.

The Latin phrase "Ad Astra Per Aspera," meaning "to the stars

> **NORTH HIGH SCHOOL**
>
> **WHAT:** Architecture
> **WHERE:** 1437 N Rochester St.
> **COST:** Free
> **PRO TIP:** The school staff offers tours of the building's interior on alumni weekend each year; however, tours inside the tower are not allowed. Call in advance to make arrangements.

Graduating seniors are the only people allowed inside the school's tower. Famous alumni include retired NFL running back Barry Sanders and two-time Olympian and Basketball Hall of Fame member Lynette Woodard.

through difficulties," appears on the tower's exterior close to an inscribed poem. The pioneer/Native American theme is depicted on the building with images of farming, the chief, hunter, and animals. Visitors are not allowed inside the tower but can walk the school's grounds to appreciate its architectural design and the nearby Minisa Bridge over the Little Arkansas River.

A poem entitled "The Tower" by Ruth Jewell appears inside the school's 1938 *Tower* yearbook. An excerpt from it reads,

> "Then twilight came,
> And I could no longer stay
> In this safe shelter.
> From the threshold of the outside world
> I looked back and behind the Tower
> Just as on the first morning—
> A symbol of strength and courage
> To keep forever in my memory."

*Parting messages from graduating seniors decorate the tower's interior walls, offset by original stained glass windows.*

# CITY FOUNDER

**Which man is responsible for establishing the city and naming it?**

The residents of Wichita have a lot for which to thank its early pioneers. These include James Richard Mead (1836–1910), from Davenport, Iowa, who moved to the area after his wife of eight years died. Ready for a new life, he sold his trading post in Towanda and relocated to acreage that would eventually become the city of Wichita in 1870. Mead was quite the entrepreneur. Not only was he considered a legendary trader with the Indians, but he also was a buffalo hunter, making him a wealthy man in his 20s. Mead conducted business with local tribes and ultimately named the city after the Wichita Indians who had occupied the territory. In May 1870, he wrote to his parents, "My main interests, however, are in Wichita. I have there 160 acres adjoining the town site which is becoming very valuable."

In 1871, he organized the Wichita and Southwestern Railroad, which made the city the place to live and do business. So much so that a sign was erected on the outskirts of town with the phrase "Everything goes in Wichita." Because of Mead's efforts, Wichita became one of the fastest-growing cities in Kansas, and it remains the largest one. The man had academic pursuits, as well. In his later years, he was president of the Kansas State Historical Society and a member of the Kansas Academy of Science.

Mead passed away on March 31, 1910, from complications of a cold that turned into pneumonia that doctors could not treat. His final resting place is in a mausoleum at the city's second-oldest cemetery, Maple Grove. Founded in 1888 by A.

---

Mead Middle School is named after the city's founder, who donated land during his lifetime for churches and school sites.

*James Mead designed his family's mausoleum from Egyptian designs.*

## MAPLE GROVE CEMETERY

**WHAT:** Mausoleum

**WHERE:** 1000 N Hillside St.

**COST:** Free

**PRO TIP:** To locate Mead's final resting place, look for a small mausoleum building near Maple Grove Cemetery's entrance.

A. Hyde and others, Maple Grove Cemetery was designed to be the "finest cemetery between the Mississippi River and the Rockies." In Mead's memoir, he wrote about the scenery where he would eventually lie in rest. "Here a vision of beauty and interest greeted our eyes, such perhaps as no other spot on the plains could furnish."

# STEEL SCULPTURE

**Which iconic public artwork serves as a symbol of the city?**

Proudly overlooking downtown Wichita, *Keeper of the Plains* is awe-inspiring. Locals know that the sculpture is the singular iconic symbol of the city, and tourists often visit it. Since 1974, the 44-foot-tall, Corten steel sculpture has remained a must-see destination at the confluence of the Big and Little Arkansas rivers. It depicts a Native American man standing with his hands raised to the Great Spirit, facing east towards the rising sun.

At its base, an outdoor plaza provides historical context to the city's Native American roots. If the setting is quiet, one can hear Native American chants from the built-in speakers in the promontory underneath it. Fire pots ignite with flames at the sculpture's base at 7 p.m. (fall and winter) or 9 p.m. (spring and summer) on good weather days.

Kansas Gas and Electric commissioned *Keeper of the Plains* for a bicentennial project celebrating the city, the Wichitennial. Kiowa-Comanche artist Francis (Blackbear) Bosin donated his work to the citizens of Wichita on May 18, 1974, at the dedication ceremony. Born in Oklahoma, Bosin came to Wichita in 1940 to work as a plate maker for Western Lithograph and as an illustrator for Boeing Aircraft. The self-taught artist also was a prolific painter who sold his works at art shows and often won awards for them. By visiting the nearby Mid-America All-Indian Museum, one can learn more about *Keeper of the Plains* artist Blackbear

---

The initial sketch of the Indian warrior sculpture was completed during the artist's recovery from heart surgery. Early versions of his sketches included tepees, spears, and feathers.

Keeper of the Plains *is framed in the background by the frame of a pedestrian bridge. The bridge's design and cable stays were designed to resemble two bows and arrows.*

Bosin and his contributions to the art world. The museum, built to resemble an arrowhead, is the site of ceremonies honoring the American Indian culture.

### KEEPER OF THE PLAINS

**WHAT:** Public art

**WHERE:** 339 Veterans Pkwy.

**COST:** Free

**PRO TIP:** Visit the original site (710 W. Douglas Ave.) of Bosin's art studio (1972–1980), now occupied by Delano BBQ. The eatery features information about the artist.

# ROWDY ROUTE

**Where did cowboys kick up their boots and saloon girls perform high kicks in cancan dresses?**

Yeehaw! Originally called Elgin, the town west of the Arkansas River, now named Delano District, was a rowdy place during the 1870s. A stop on the Chisholm Trail, Wichita was home to holding pens used by cattle drivers from Texas when they pushed herds through town. And when the cowboys were not working, they lived a lifestyle of partying and debauchery. The town did not have a sheriff, so it quickly resembled a scene from the Wild West. The violence in Delano was so prevalent that injured cowboys were taken to the Wichita Hospital, which stood on the northwest corner of Douglas Avenue and Seneca Street.

The saloons were bustling with gunslingers ready to gamble and drink into the night. Unruly cowboys bet on the Running of the Doves, an event featuring naked women running from the river to town at high speeds. Of course, other forms of money-making took place in Delano. Prostitution flourished in hotels and boardinghouses where women of the night conducted business.

The town was an active place to work and play until it wasn't. When the cattle trade moved west to Dodge City, Delano was incorporated into the city of Wichita in 1880.

Now, the historic neighborhood is home to retail stores, locally owned restaurants, and stylish office buildings. Hand-painted

## HISTORIC DELANO DISTRICT

**WHAT:** Neighborhood

**WHERE:** Douglas Avenue west of the Arkansas River

**COST:** Free

**PRO TIP:** At The Monarch (579 W Douglas Ave.), enjoy a Running Doves Reuben stacked with smoked corned beef and sauerkraut on rye bread. Keep with the Delano theme and order a glass of whiskey—they claim to have the largest selection in the state.

*Now a desired destination for shopping and dining, the Historic Delano District was once home to saloons, cowboys, cattle, and lawless activities.*

murals illustrating scenes from the early Wild West days are visible on the sides of buildings. Insignia sidewalk pavers and bike racks are imprinted with symbols representing the Chisholm Trail, the river, and trees in the Delano business district.

---

People who wanted to cross the Douglas Avenue Bridge over the Arkansas River in 1872 were charged a toll, which didn't go over well with citizens. In 1877, the city and county resolved the matter by purchasing the bridge, eliminating the need to charge a toll.

# EVER THE ECCENTRIC

**What becomes of metal pieces, a broken toy, and a light sconce?**

One might call Gary Pendergrass a tinkerer—the ultimate recycler of junk. Call him what you will; he is a master of making artistic creations. The retired home remodeler spends his days sorting through massive collections of metal parts and plastic pieces to design sculptures for others to enjoy. In 2013, Steampunk Village took shape after Pendergrass discovered an appreciation for the Victorian era–, steam-powered industrial design. The gauges. The gears. Each part, when combined with another, takes on a new identity. Musical instruments become body parts. HVAC tubing transforms into train parts. A lamp's base serves as an animal's nose. Sometimes he is inspired by an object he collects, or that someone gives him. A weekly check of a nearby dump trailer usually produces items for inspiration.

On occasion, he works on a commissioned piece for someone. The process is labor-intensive. Pendergrass creates multiple versions using models made often using Mountain Dew box material before finishing a piece using sourced objects. Gone are the days of working with wood—it doesn't last as long as metal.

Pendergrass's creations show the artist's infinite imagination. Metal dragons and a miniature Statue of Liberty tower over passersby, but the residents of his west Wichita neighborhood don't seem to mind. In fact, drivers are encouraged to park and take a self-guided tour of Steampunk Village.

---

The operation becomes a family affair during Halloween, when Pendergrass and his brother pass out candy dressed in homemade, one-of-a-kind costumes.

*Lucky Steampunk Village visitors are sometimes invited into Gary Pendergrass's workshop and private home for a behind-the-scenes tour. The artist lives across the street, with a direct view of his creations.*

## STEAMPUNK VILLAGE

**WHAT:** Public Art
**WHERE:** 3831 W 17th St. N
**COST:** Free
**PRO TIP:** Visit Steampunk Village during the day to get the best glimpse of the artwork. Park on 17th St. in front of the village to avoid blocking the neighbors' driveways.

The artist may be on-site, and he's always happy to meet fans of his work. As one approaches the driveway, they should listen for the sound of metalsmithing at work and yell, "Hello?!" If he doesn't respond, he encourages visitors to call the phone number on the sign that reads "Welcome. Be Careful & Safe."

# PRESERVED PLANE

**Why is an aircraft permanently at rest in the middle of downtown?**

It's not every day that you walk by an airplane parked in the middle of downtown, but then again, you may not be walking in the middle of the Air Capital of the World. Adjacent to the surplus store The Yard in Wichita, the Twin Beech is stationed in a pocket park surrounded by fencing, on view for passersby to appreciate. The plane was built by Beech Aircraft Corporation in Wichita. It was used by the Army Air Corps in 1943 and was one of more than 7,000 Model 18s produced during World War II. Like a good soldier, the aircraft hopped among training commands, serving at bases in Texas and Nebraska.

It came to rest at its current location after the family-run business made it a priority to preserve and park the plane there. As they say, the "monument is The Yard's gift to Wichita, a fitting reminder of all who have worked in the aircraft industry and a fitting tribute to all who served during World War II and other con flights." According to The Yard's website, the "Twin Beech became a C-45G Expeditor transport. It was the first remanufactured Twin Beech delivered to the Air Force, earning it manufacturer's number AF-1, as in Air Force One."

---

Beech Aircraft was founded in Wichita in 1932 by Walter and Olive Beech. The first Beech design was the Model 17, a biplane with a staggered wing design that could travel up to 200 miles per hour.

*A metal plaque, "Air Force One, the First One," is on display near the airplane, noting that the US government purchased thousands of Model 18s from Beech Aircraft in Wichita.*

The Yard is a hidden treasure in its own right. Tinkerers and hobbyists are regulars, hunting for supplies ranging from rope and aircraft parts to file cabinets and steel tubing. Whatever you need to get a project done, they sell it.

## ORIGINAL AF-1

**WHAT:** Airplane

**WHERE:** The Yard, 725 E Central Ave.

**COST:** Free

**PRO TIP:** While shopping at The Yard, walk outside the main building to peruse the extra buildings that house large-scale parts and supplies.

# MOOD FLAGS

**What kind of day is it at work today?**

She was an aviation pioneer. A chairwoman. And a boss who didn't keep her feelings a secret. In fact, if you walked near Olive Ann Beech's office at Beech Aircraft, the flags outside her door indicated what kind of day it was. The flag with the sun communicated that she was in a good mood. She was not having the best day if the storm clouds flag was in the primary position. Al Higdon, a former communications executive at Beech and Learjet, once wrote in the *Wichita Eagle*, "When the miniature 'Oh, Happy Day' flag was in place about her office doorway, signifying something good had happened, you knew things might be a bit more relaxed. Absent this sighting, you entered her office with caution."

Visitors to Kansas Aviation Museum's Women of Aviation exhibit can view Beech's office flags firsthand. The first floor of the museum includes information about her career.

Born in Waverly, Kansas, Beech defied gender roles at an early age and had a bank account by age seven. In her early 20s, she attended business school and began a career in aviation. She transitioned from bookkeeper to office manager and eventually assumed the role of Beech Aircraft company president after her husband, Walter, died in 1950. Before retiring in 1982, she earned top awards, including the title of one of the 10 highest-ranking women executives in major American corporations.

Not known for giving frequent interviews, she was quick to share her enthusiasm for the aircraft industry and its future. As reported by Kansas Public Radio, she said, "If you enjoy

---

Walter H. and Olive Ann Beech lie in rest inside Old Mission Mausoleum, 3424 E 21st St. N.

*Olive Ann Beech's flags are displayed in the Women of Aviation exhibit at the Kansas Aviation Museum.*

your work, all you have to do is be capable and take the pitfalls along with the good. I was very fortunate throughout my life that I didn't have to do anything that I didn't like. I enjoyed what I did."

And on those days, you can only imagine the "Oh, Happy Day" flag was positioned outside her office door.

## KANSAS AVIATION MUSEUM EXHIBIT

**WHAT:** Exhibit

**WHERE:** Kansas Aviation Museum, 3350 S George Washington Blvd.

**COST:** $10 for adults, $8 for seniors (55+), $6 for children 4–12, free for children 3 and under

**PRO TIP:** Visit Wichita State University's Special Collections and University Archives to gain supervised access to Walter H. and Olive Ann Beech's collection, which includes correspondence, scrapbooks, photographs, and memos, most of which focus on Mrs. Beech's life and career.

# TREE TUNNEL

**What is the use of an above-ground tunnel on the city's east side?**

A naturally made path under a canopy of trees at Chisholm Creek Park is an attraction for residents and visitors to the city who learn of it. Trailblazers seek out the Tunnel of Trees for its natural, whimsical design. Photographers use the passageway to frame their subjects for portraits.

Chisholm Creek Park has several paths for nature lovers to enjoy, but the Tunnel of Trees distinguishes itself from the others. The forest develops a chartreuse color in spring, eventually transitioning to a darker green as the days pass. In summer, the tunnel creates a shaded path to escape the sweltering Kansas sun, if only for a few minutes. During autumn, the leaves fall, leaving behind dark, barren branches.

Aside from the tunnel, Chisholm Creek Park is a natural oasis in the center of a bustling city. The sound of the nearby K-96 state highway fades as one walks further along the park's paths. Considered one of the largest parks in Wichita, it serves as a habitat to waterfowl, deer, and native animals on 282

### TUNNEL OF TREES

**WHAT:** Tunnel

**WHERE:** Chisholm Creek Park

**COST:** Free

**PRO TIP:** Leave your dog at home. Pets are not allowed on the trail leading to the Tunnel of Trees. Look for designated pet-friendly trail markers in other areas of the park.

---

Chisholm Creek Park is home to 38 species of trees and shrubs.

*The Tunnel of Trees is an unmarked, well-traveled trail. To find it, enter the North Oliver St. entrance and access 1.7 miles of the Cottonwood Trail.*

acres. Visitors can explore 2.5 miles of paved trails navigating through native prairie, with clearings opening up to Island Pond and wetlands. Nestled in the park, the Great Plains Nature Center invites people to learn about plant and animal species.

# STATION SIGN

**Why is a Wichita sign located above the downtown corridor?**

Union Station's railway was a gateway for passenger trains arriving and departing via Wichita in the early 1900s. Santa Fe, Rock Island, Frisco, and Orient railroad companies used it. The construction of Union Station started in July 1912 and was completed in March 1914. What was the price tag of the project? $2,500,000. The elevated track divides the city's Old Town district and the downtown corridor. The railway platform sign represents a time in the city's history when enterprise flourished and marked the station's location.

During the opening day celebration of Union Station on March 7, 1914, it was reported in the *Wichita Eagle* that Senator Long spoke to a crowd and said, "They may marvel at this, but no other

*Passenger rail service to Wichita's Union Station ended in 1979, but the railroad platform's sign remains a symbol of its history.*

town in Kansas is entitled to such a magnificent station." Mayor W. J. Babb also addressed people in attendance and remarked, "Wichita is the best city by far of any in Kansas, and of which the state is justly proud." He called Wichita "the Queen City of the Southwest."

Today, Union Station Plaza consists of office space. Built in 1887, the nearby Rock Island Depot now houses restaurants. Railroad enthusiasts can tour the Great Plains Transportation Museum, located across the street from Union Station Plaza, where steam locomotives and restored train cars sit on display.

## UNION STATION PLAZA

**WHAT:** Railway platform sign

**WHERE:** 701 E Douglas Ave.

**COST:** Free

**PRO TIP:** To take a photo of the railroad platform sign, walk up the hill on the south end of Union Station Plaza or access it as a visitor of the Great Plains Transportation Museum.

---

On the day Union Station opened, it had a soda fountain, check room, and dining room. Women were asked to remove their hats before entering the dining room during that evening's banquet so guests could see the after-dinner speakers.

# GAS STATION GRUB

**Where can you go to fuel up on food in a place that used to sell gas?**

When a building's rich history dates back to its days as a full-service filling station and garage built in 1931, you preserve its history. During the station's heyday, the downtown district consisted of a collection of warehouses of various industries. It's become a mixed-use neighborhood with retail stores, hotels, offices, apartments, and restaurants like the Pumphouse. The garage-to-bar concept keeps with the building's service station theme. Since the 1930s, it has remained locally owned and operated. The building's interior is thoughtfully designed and features wall art and neon signs with a nod to the drive-in service station era. A vintage gas pump is positioned next to a row of metal lockers. Like the original building, its garage doors open, allowing fresh air to flow into the space during warm weather days. The Greenhouse patio, featuring lounge seating, is cooled with misters or warmed with heaters to keep patrons comfortable.

Patrons can sip on cocktails at the bar, including one that is served from a gas pump handle. The drink menu, a.k.a. Lubrication Service, allows guests to choose a

### PUMPHOUSE

**WHAT:** Bar and grill

**WHERE:** 825 E 2nd St. N

**COST:** $4.99–$20.99

**PRO TIP:** For a laid-back experience, visit the Pumphouse during daytime hours to watch the game and enjoy a meal. The bar and grill takes on a nightclub vibe after the sun goes down.

---

*A repurposed oil pit is viewable via a plexiglass floor, which holds wine bottles.*

specialty drink by its octane rating. Hungry diners can park themselves at a table or choose a bar seat to enjoy the Pumphouse Deluxe burger, Full Service specialty pizza, or a daily lunch special.

Where should diners park their vehicles before entering the bar and grill? Free parking is available in close-by surface lots within walking distance of the Pumphouse. The Old Town Parking Garage at 215 N Mosley St. is another no-cost option for two-hour parking.

*The Pumphouse is a transformed, full-service automotive station that serves drinks and food in the heart of historic Old Town.*

27

# SAVED BY THE BELL

**Where can the public view three floors of items used by the school district, dating back to 1873?**

Built in 1890 during economic progress in the city, McCormick Elementary is Wichita's oldest public school building and the only one designed by the architectural firm of Proudfoot and Bird. Listed as a national landmark today, it opened with 33 students and four teachers. The area looked quite different at the time. Kids who lived in the country walked through fields and muddy roads to get to school.

In later years, additions were made to the original four-room building to include more classrooms, an auditorium, and offices. But the school bell rang for the last time in 1992 when it closed due to declining enrollment. Now, it is a museum filled with remarkable relics of the school district's past.

*McCormick Elementary School is named after John McCormick, an early Wichita settler.*

---

Some of the school's students went on to work in education, including Florence Laidlaw Williams, a first-grader in 1891, who later taught at McCormick Elementary.

Dedicated volunteers organize, clean, and display curated items on view to museumgoers.

The building itself is an artifact. Many of the original school's relics still exist, including water buckets and dippers where students would hydrate inside the main entrance. Lab equipment dating back to 1923 sits untouched in the science room. Above the desk in the principal's office hangs a paddle on the wall. If students felt ill, they would cross the wood-floored hallway to the nurse's office.

A walk through the hallways reveals display cases containing tarnished trophies, letter jackets, and photographs. Old classrooms are filled with archived photos and books, including the largest selection of high school yearbooks, which serve as a research library for visitors who make an appointment.

How does the old school remain open to visitors? When Museum Programs were cut from the Wichita Unified School District 259 budget in 1997, the building was closed. In December of that same year, the Wichita Association of Retired School Personnel voted to accept the challenge of reopening McCormick School Museum as a community service project. Monies raised through grants, fundraising events, and donations keep the city's oldest school building's doors open and the lights on. Fundraising events such as Kansas Day Chili Feed, Boiler-Made Potato Bake in March, and the Christmas Open House draw crowds.

---

**MCCORMICK SCHOOL MUSEUM**

**WHAT:** Building

**WHERE:** 855 S Martinson St.

**COST:** Free, "Keep the Bell Ringing" donations accepted

**PRO TIP:** Experience what it was like to ring the school's bell. Ask a tour guide if you can pull the rope, located on the first floor and connected to the bell.

# WHISTLE-STOP WONDER

**Why do miniature trains make such a big impression?**

What looks like a typical building in downtown Wichita is nothing of the sort. Wichita Toy Train Club & Museum is home to entire towns, mountains with ski lifts, and carnivals. Model train lovers of all ages appreciate each of its rooms, featuring tables of locomotives running through multi-level layouts and landscapes miniature in scale. As each train roars along a stretch of track, museumgoers watch as it follows the path up and down hills and through handcrafted tunnels. Like real-life trains, the toy locomotives emit steam, and whistles break the silence. The museum is operated by the Wichita Toy Train Club, a group of dedicated model train enthusiasts who spend countless hours tinkering with setups and running runs. Visitors are welcome to take a self-guided tour, and club members are eager to answer questions about train layouts. Every tree, rock, figurine, and most of the model train layout accessories are handcrafted by club members. Curious about how each train operates? They are

## WICHITA TOY TRAIN CLUB & MUSEUM

**WHAT:** Museum

**WHERE:** 130 S Laura St.

**COST:** $7 for adults, $4 for youth, free for children ages 5 and under

**PRO TIP:** The model train setup makes it easy to become mesmerized. Plan at least 30 minutes to one hour to enjoy the museum to avoid losing track of time.

---

The museum includes multiple rooms containing train layouts, including one set up in a low-lit room, allowing its night scene to illuminate the room.

*The model train layouts are designed by the museum's club members, organized in 1985. Their first major project was designing and building a 12-foot-by-16-foot model train layout for the Children's Museum of Wichita.*

happy to give visitors a look under the platform while pointing out elaborate wiring systems.

Once a year, the museum participates in the Wichita Model Train Show, where vendors buy, sell, and trade model train gear. They are known for taking some of the museum's layouts to events. The fun continues at the museum when they host kids' birthday parties. Children can learn how to run trains, and the birthday boy or girl is gifted with a T-shirt or train whistle.

31

# STELLAR STONE

**Why are 14-foot limestone rocks positioned in a pattern in a park?**

Walk through Central Riverside Park, and one may notice something unique protruding from the ground. Sometimes referred to as Wichita's Mini Stonehenge, limestone pillars covered in colorful tiles serve as a solar calendar.

The sun's location aligns the stones at sunrise, noon, and sunset. During the summer solstice, the prime time to visit the solar calendar, the sun travels the longest path through the sky, serving as the longest day with sunlight. A three-inch glass orb in a stone on the ground near the solar calendar glows when the sun reaches its highest point in the sky.

What is the difference between a solar calendar and a sundial? Both inventions mark the sun's position, but a solar calendar indicates the time of year versus the time of day, like a sundial. A solar calendar also helps determine the season by the position of the sun relative to the stars.

---

**CENTRAL RIVERSIDE PARK**

**WHAT:** Solar Calendar

**WHERE:** 720 Nims St.

**COST:** Free

**PRO TIP:** To view a ceramic tile mural by Murillo, visit *Music's Magic* at 1330 E Douglas Ave. The mural contains 25,000 bits of glass and weighs 3,000 pounds.

---

A three-inch glass orb in a stone on the ground near the solar calendar glows when the sun is at its highest point in the sky.

*The blue orb atop the standing stone aligns with three ground stones.*

    A group of area artists, led by Steve Murillo and Terry Corbett, designed and installed the solar calendar in May 2003 as a part of the city's renovation of the Riverside Park system. Corbett created the tiled Aztec, Mayan, and celestial scenes on the stone facades. Parkgoers can appreciate the artists' creation year-round, as Central Riverside Park is open from dawn to dusk.

# SCI-FI SCULPTURE

**Why is a robot buried underground at Wichita State University?**

One of over 80 sculptures on the campus of Wichita State University, *The Celestial Mechanic*, 2016–2018, by artist Randy Regier often surprises passersby because they're not expecting it. The cartoon-looking robot sits in a coffin-like box under a tempered glass window exposed above Earth's surface.

The American artist's sculpture may raise questions. Why a robot? Why is it buried in the dirt facing the sky? Influenced by articles showcasing artifacts found in Kansas that you wouldn't expect to find, Regier was inspired to create *The Celestial Mechanic* as it appears today. As Regier said during a 2019 speech at the university, "Are we dreaming about the past? Are we dreaming about the future? Are we balancing the two? It's a line I obviously tell in my work."

*The Celestial Mechanic* was dedicated into the Martin H. Bush Outdoor Sculpture Collection in 2019. Regier noted during his speech, "I love writing stories, but I don't have the patience to write the written word, only to read it . . . I'm a writer who uses objects to write in many cases."

To access the sculpture, park your car in the student and visitor parking south of WuShock Drive near the Sheldon Coleman Tennis Complex and walk north to the art installation.

---

The *Celestial Mechanic* was inspired by the book *Fallen Spaceman* by Lee Harding, and Regier used curated items from antique shops to create it.

*The artist refers to the robot as a "she" and made her from domestic items found in Kansas.*

## WICHITA STATE UNIVERSITY

**WHAT:** Sculpture

**WHERE:** Located between Ahlberg Hall and the Engineering Building

**COST:** Free

**PRO TIP:** Download the Smartify app and use your phone's camera to scan the campus sculptures to learn more about them.

# GO GLAZY

**Where in the city are there over a dozen reasons to be happy?**

What did it feel like to walk into an amusement park for the first time? The games, the rides, the delicious concession food? Walking into The Donut Whole feels a bit like that, plus the place smells like freshly baked cake donuts.

The donut shop isn't hard to find. A gigantic rooster statue named Ed sits atop the donut shop's roof and is designed to attract attention. Inside, a massive fiberglass lion from Joyland Amusement Park is displayed across a glass case filled with hand-glazed donuts. A wall of pinball games invites game players to earn a high score. Colorful paintings by local artists adorn the hallway walls. A giant tiger face, another Joyland artifact, is next to a handprinted piano in the front room.

Donuts are topped with mouthwatering ingredients guaranteed to satisfy one's sugar fix. Berry Crunch is sprinkled with Fruity Pebbles™ cereal.

---

### THE DONUT WHOLE

**WHAT:** Bakery

**WHERE:** 1720 E Douglas Ave.

**COST:** $2–$6

**PRO TIP:** Miss the days of Joyland? Visit the ice cream shop, Churn and Burn, at 548 S Oliver St. to view original signage and framed photography of the bygone amusement park.

---

The donut shop is celebrity-approved. In 2014, Food Network celebrity Alton Brown ate powdered sugar donuts at the bakery during his Edible Inevitable Tour.

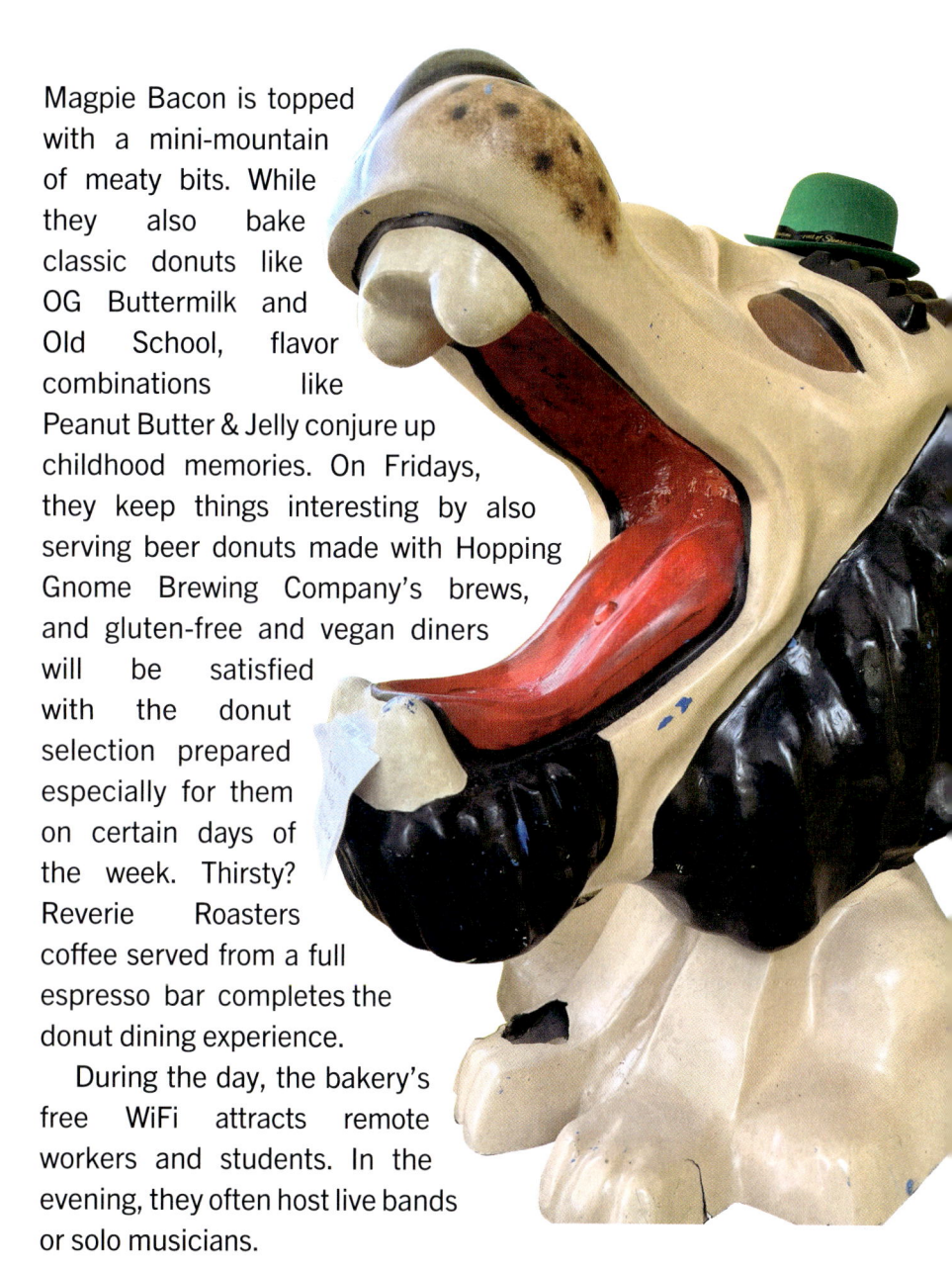

Magpie Bacon is topped with a mini-mountain of meaty bits. While they also bake classic donuts like OG Buttermilk and Old School, flavor combinations like Peanut Butter & Jelly conjure up childhood memories. On Fridays, they keep things interesting by also serving beer donuts made with Hopping Gnome Brewing Company's brews, and gluten-free and vegan diners will be satisfied with the donut selection prepared especially for them on certain days of the week. Thirsty? Reverie Roasters coffee served from a full espresso bar completes the donut dining experience.

During the day, the bakery's free WiFi attracts remote workers and students. In the evening, they often host live bands or solo musicians.

*Once a fixture of Joyland Amusement Park, a tiger statue greets customers in the bakery.*

# PATH FORWARD

**What lies at the end of the yellow brick road?**

Dorothy of *The Wizard of Oz* knew that Kansas was where she was meant to be, and it meant following the yellow brick road; then, it was one ruby jeweled shoe in front of the other until she reached home.

One can follow the yellow brick road at O. J. Watson Park on the city's south side, just as Dorothy did. Munchkins don't border the road. And Glinda the Good Witch isn't present. But if one feels inclined to dance or skip down the yellow path singing, "Follow the Yellow Brick Road," it's the next best thing to the fictional movie scene. The route starts near the park's concession stand.

The "magical" path didn't appear like a movie prop without hours of labor. Over a dozen workers installed the path by hand, brick by brick, after leveling the ground beneath with sand.

Some say the yellow brick road is a metaphor for following the path one identifies as the best option, the best route to accomplish a goal. If feeling happy while enjoying nature is the immediate goal, O. J. Watson Park checks all the

### O. J. WATSON PARK

**WHAT:** Path

**WHERE:** 3022 S McLean Blvd.

**COST:** Admission to the park is free, but fees are charged for some park activities.

**PRO TIP:** The paved brick road is 1/8 mile and loops through a section of the park, so be prepared for a walk.

---

O. J. Watson Park once featured life-size wooden sculptures of *Wizard of Oz* characters, but they were removed due to vandalism.

*Artist Katherine Conrad painted the mural near the brick-lined path. She started by sketching the scene before painting over it.*

boxes. Adjacent to the yellow-brick-lined path is a colorful mural depicting the characters from the movie, an ideal backdrop for a family photo. Other fun activities at the park include a miniature golf course, stable featuring pony rides, a fishing lake, train rides, and sand volleyball. Prefer to see the park from the water? Ask about renting a kayak or pedal boat.

# FIT FOR ROYALTY

**What lies beyond the doors of an enchanting castle near the river?**

Historically, castles have been home to people of nobility. The Campbell Castle, located in the Riverside neighborhood, was built from 1886 to 1888 in Romanesque style by Colonel Burton Harvey Campbell and his wife, Ellen. He was an upstate New Yorker who came to Kansas and prospered as a cattle rancher. After one year in Hutchinson, they settled in Wichita in 1881.

On nearly two acres of land, Colonel Campbell built a single-family home unlike any other in the city at its time. According to historical documents, it took architects two years to complete the design plans. The couple spared no expense in sourcing materials for the castle's construction. The exterior consists of rough-cut limestone, and its circular tower, with bird's-eye views of the city, is built with a checkerboard pattern.

The stately home is almost 15,000 square feet and includes a two-story carriage house. Combined, both buildings have 17 bedrooms and 19 private bathrooms. The home's interior is lavish, featuring nine fireplaces, hand-carved fretwork, staircases, and floors made of mahogany, walnut, oak, and cherry wood.

---

### CAMPBELL CASTLE

**WHAT:** House

**WHERE:** 1155 N River Blvd.

**COST:** It's free to view the exterior of the castle at a respectful distance, as it is a private residence.

**PRO TIP:** To view the landmark residence from its exterior, use nearby on-street parking and walk along the sidewalk surrounding it.

---

During the writing of this book, the home was listed for sale at $3.5 million on Zillow.com. It was once used as a bed and breakfast, Castle Inn Riverside.

*The Campbell Castle is listed on the local, state, and national Registers of Historic Places.*

Other ornate design features include German stained glass, a grand staircase, and an arched dining room window imported from London, England. The Campbell family enjoyed a scenic view of the Little Arkansas River from the east-facing windows and an open rooftop area. Other leisurely activities most likely included reading in the library or eating breakfast in the solarium.

# COLORFUL CREATION

**When is it okay to walk on top of an artist's work?**

The Wichita Art Museum is known for housing unique exhibits, but it's not every day that museum patrons are encouraged to take off their shoes and walk on top of an artist's creation. Well, sort of.

In an area on the museum's second floor, visitors can step onto a transparent, thick surface showcasing multicolored glass forms underneath. The in-floor artistic masterpiece *Persian Seaform Installation*, created by internationally renowned artist Dale Chihuly, is also viewable from the first floor's lobby. As museumgoers enter the building, they can look up to see 400 flowery platters and bowls made to resemble sea creatures. *Persian Seaform Installation* took four days to install and was part of the museum's $10.5 million expansion project in 2003.

Installing the piece was an intricate process. The 1,500-pound sculpture was constructed in an airtight case because lighting could create dangerous

---

## WICHITA ART MUSEUM

**WHAT:** Sculpture

**WHERE:** 1400 W Museum Blvd.

**COST:** Free admission

**PRO TIP:** *Confetti Chandelier* serves as a colorful backdrop for photos. The hall hosts events at the museum, and its windows provide views of a ground-level sculpture garden.

---

The Wichita Art Museum has more than one blown glass sculpture on display by American-born artist Dale Chihuly. The artist began his career as a weaver and studied at University of Washington.

Persian Seaform Installation *is popular with the museum's youngest visitors. Dale Chihuly's avant-garde glass sculptures on display at the museum represent a fraction of the artist's work on display in 200 museum collections worldwide.*

heat. When the display requires cleaning, each piece has to be delicately removed, cleaned, and replaced atop another piece.

Another Chihuly piece created in 2003, *Confetti Chandelier*, is a commissioned glass sculpture hanging from the second-floor ceiling in the Great Hall. The massive glass piece is comprised of 600 hand-blown glass balloons attached to a frame.

# SIGNIFICANT SIGN

**Why did a road in the city become a cattle highway?**

The Chisholm Trail historical marker was placed at the corner of Douglas Avenue and McLean Boulevard in 1941 by the Kansas United Spanish War Veterans. The location is significant, as Wichita was part of the cattle drive route from Texas through Kansas in the 1860s. Texas cattle selling only for one to two dollars per head commanded a higher price in northern states: thus, the "cattle highway" was formed.

How did the route get its name? One man's ability to serve as a peacemaker between tribes and settlers made it possible. Jesse Chisholm, of Scottish-Cherokee ancestry, built trade relationships with the Wichita, Kiowa, Comanche, and Osage native tribes. He served as a peacemaker between tribes and settlers and was referred to as the Ambassador of the Plains. He established the cattle drive trail that supplied Texas cattle to northern towns.

Chisholm laid out the trail between his trading post at the mouth of the Little Arkansas River to the Indian territory that extended northward to Abilene, Kansas. Cowboys pushed cattle herds through town and across the river near the Douglas Avenue Bridge.

In later years, Chisholm worked as a trader with the Indians. Although illiterate, Jesse Chisholm spoke several languages and served as an interpreter for the Republic of Texas and the United States government during the creation of treaties

---

The neighborhood west known as the Delano District was once "a place of drunkenness, gambling, and gunplay," according to the township marker placed by Wichita's Historic Preservation Board in 1993.

*The Chisholm Trail (1865–1874) marker was erected in 1941. A history of the Delano township is inscribed on the east-facing side of it.*

## CHISHOLM TRAIL

**WHAT:** Historical marker

**WHERE:** Douglas Ave. and McLean Blvd.

**COST:** Free

**PRO TIP:** Walk west to the clock tower *Window in Time*, located in the Historic Delano District's roundabout, for a closer look at its panels detailing scenes from the Chisholm Trail. A time capsule was buried at its base.

with Native American tribes. Chisholm eventually opened salt mines north of Geary, Oklahoma. He died of cholera on March 4, 1868, before the peak of the cattle drives.

    The Delano District, located west of where the historical marker sits today, was once considered a bustling cattle town. In the 1870s, cowboys stopped there along their cattle drive route to enjoy saloons, brothels, and gambling houses. Gunfights often took place in the street. Because of the lack of law enforcement, the area grew into a prosperous business district. Today, that area, considered one of Wichita's oldest neighborhoods, consists of retail shops, art galleries, and restaurants.

# ORNATE OFFICE

**Which man's work space is preserved for visitors to admire, over 130 years later?**

John B. Carey wasn't the first mayor. However, he was mayor in 1892, the same year the mayor's office in City Hall opened. But unlike other mayors, he is the only one to have an office preserved for people to admire from behind a velvet rope at Wichita-Sedgwick County Historical Museum. The building, built as the city's original City Hall in 1892, showcases the mayor's office on the third floor.

The room that served as his office is complete with period furniture, lighting, and vintage books. One can almost imagine Carey signing essential documents and penning letters at his desk. Perhaps he took breaks from his duties to peer through the windows that overlooked Main and Williams streets. Did he spin the antique globe? Did he chew tobacco and use the ornate spittoon?

Serving from 1891–1892, Mayor Carey was a prominent businessman. When the *Weekly Eagle* reporter interviewed him about what policy he would pursue while in office, he replied, "It will be one of honesty and economy. I intend to shut down on doodlers and economize on everything." A year later, after serving in office, he delivered on his promise to help promote the city's economy by building The Carey House in 1886 and 1887, a five-story luxury hotel that would gain nationwide recognition after Carry Nation destroyed its bar in December 1900. Today, the building is Eaton Place.

---

The city's first mayor, Edward Bird Allen, was elected in 1871. During this time, mayoral terms were one year, and the City Council appointed the mayor.

A limestone bust of Mayor John Carey is visible near the north entrance of the Wichita-Sedgwick County Historical Museum, the city's original City Hall. It was added after the original gargoyle was damaged during construction.

## WICHITA-SEDGWICK COUNTY HISTORICAL MUSEUM

**WHAT:** Exhibit

**WHERE:** 204 S Main St.

**COST:** Museum Admission

**PRO TIP:** Walk east on Douglas Avenue to St. Francis Ave. to get a closer look at the mayor's one-time hotel, now renamed Eaton Place.

The man who originally immigrated from Ireland to Illinois and later to Wichita in 1874 died at his home in San Jose, California, at age 71. He prospered in the lumber business, forming the Carey Lumber Company, before becoming a councilman and mayor. Even during his final days, Carey thought fondly about the city. In the obituary in the *Weekly Eagle* on November 24, 1899, a reporter wrote, "His love of the city was indicated in one of his letters, in which he indicated his wish to be able to return to Wichita, that he might end his life there."

# DESIGNED TO SHINE

**How does one man's trash become another man's treasure?**

What could an artist make from a pile of discarded car bumpers? Animals, of course. American artist John Walter Kearney was known for life-size welding sculptures. One day while at a Cape Cod salvage yard, the Omaha-born sculptor was inspired to create art using car parts. He got to work using his welding skills learned on the job as a United States Navy sailor during World War II.

Several of his chrome creations dot the city's downtown landscape. A horse with an authoritative posture stands in front of the Ruffin Building. A metallic pig and giraffe tower make their home inside.

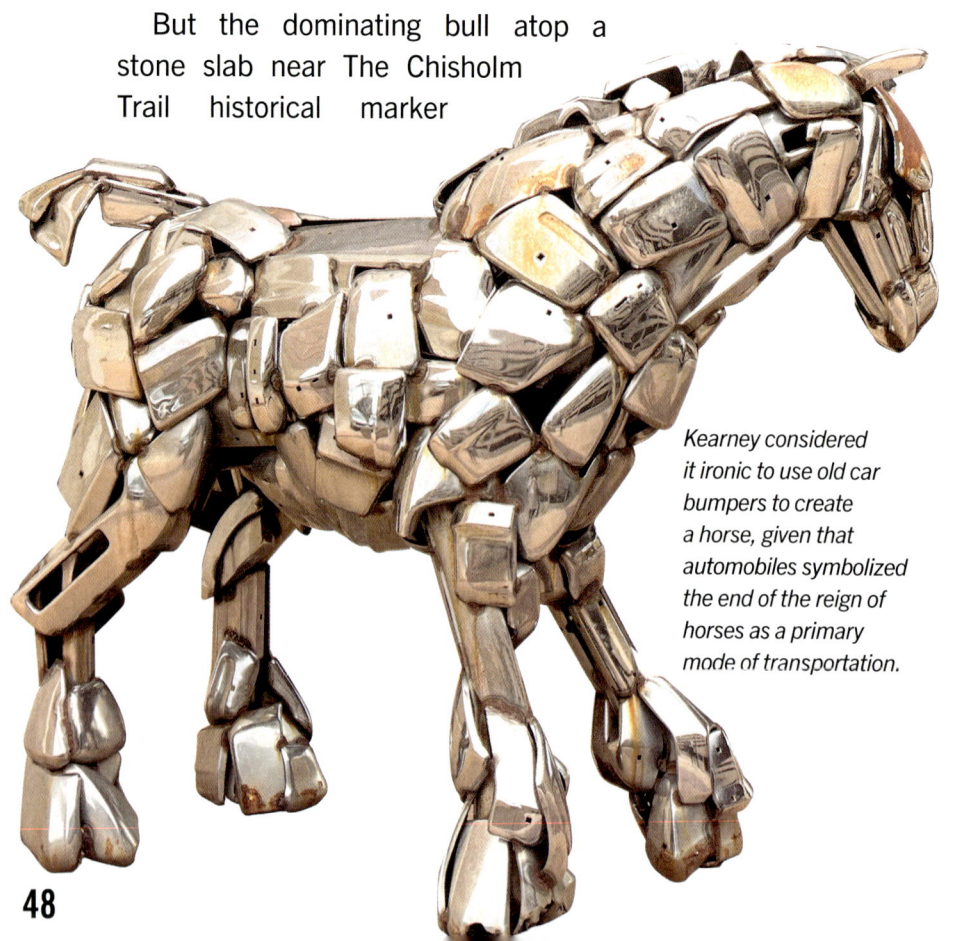

But the dominating bull atop a stone slab near The Chisholm Trail historical marker

*Kearney considered it ironic to use old car bumpers to create a horse, given that automobiles symbolized the end of the reign of horses as a primary mode of transportation.*

48

on the edge of the Historic Delano District tends to draw the most attention for its symbolism. Part of Kearney's *Two Steers*, the shiny bull is more than another public art piece. It represents cowboys' cattle drives along the Chisholm Trail from Texas through Kansas.

The second steer is located on the Maize South High School campus. Both steers were initially commissioned pieces for the 1978 Kansas Coliseum opening. For the 100-piece sculpture, the artist used 1,000 pounds of bumpers.

The artist did see his creations installed when he visited Wichita for a one-day exhibition of his work in 1984. That same year, his chrome bumper creations sold for at least $2,200.

Kearney passed away in 2014 at age 89, but not before spending over three decades creating chrome bumper sculptures. His work exists in museums and public spaces across the nation.

> **CHROME BUMPER SCULPTURES**
>
> **WHAT:** Public art
>
> **WHERE:** Various locations in the city
>
> **COST:** Free
>
> **PRO TIP:** Visit the Ruffin Building, 100 N Broadway St., to see the most animal sculptures by Kearney in one location in the city.

---

One of the artist's sculptures, *Grandfather's Horse*, is located on the main campus of Wichita State University, west of Hubbard Hall. It was Kearney's tribute to his great-grandfather, a founder of Coffeyville, Kansas.

# LADY LIBERTY

**Why is a replica of the Statue of Liberty located in the city?**

A replica of the Statue of Liberty stands with a torch in hand on the west end of East High School's 44-acre urban campus. Drivers hurrying to and from downtown might miss it if they don't keep their eyes peeled for it.

The eight-foot-tall statue was erected on the campus in 1951 during United Nations Week. The dedication ceremony, led by Wichita Bar Association Chairman Henry V. Gott, included about 500 people in attendance. It rests on an 11-point star base made of sandstone. The plaque reads, "The Boy Scouts of America dedicate this copy of the Statue of Liberty as a pledge of everlasting fidelity and loyalty."

Why was a miniature Lady Liberty installed in the heart of the Midwest? It was created by the Boy Scouts of America as part of the Crusade to Strengthen the Arm of Liberty, launched in 1949. Referred to as Liberty Sisters, the statues exist in 39 states and territories in the United States. As a symbol of

---

**EAST HIGH SCHOOL**

**WHAT:** Statue

**WHERE:** 2301 E Douglas Ave.

**COST:** Free

**PRO TIP:** Visit the Boy Scouts of America Statue of Liberty Replicas Facebook page to view photos of statues nationwide.

---

The first Liberty Sister replica was dedicated on November 20, 1949, in Kansas City. J. P. Whitaker, the founder of the crusade, was a Kansas City businessman and one-time Boy Scouts of America Commissioner in the city.

freedom, the East High School campus statue serves as a reminder of Liberty's challenge. It is one of about 200 Lady Liberty replica statues in America.

*A miniature Statue of Liberty stands proud on the original campus of Roosevelt Middle School, which merged with East High School, the home of the Blue Aces.*

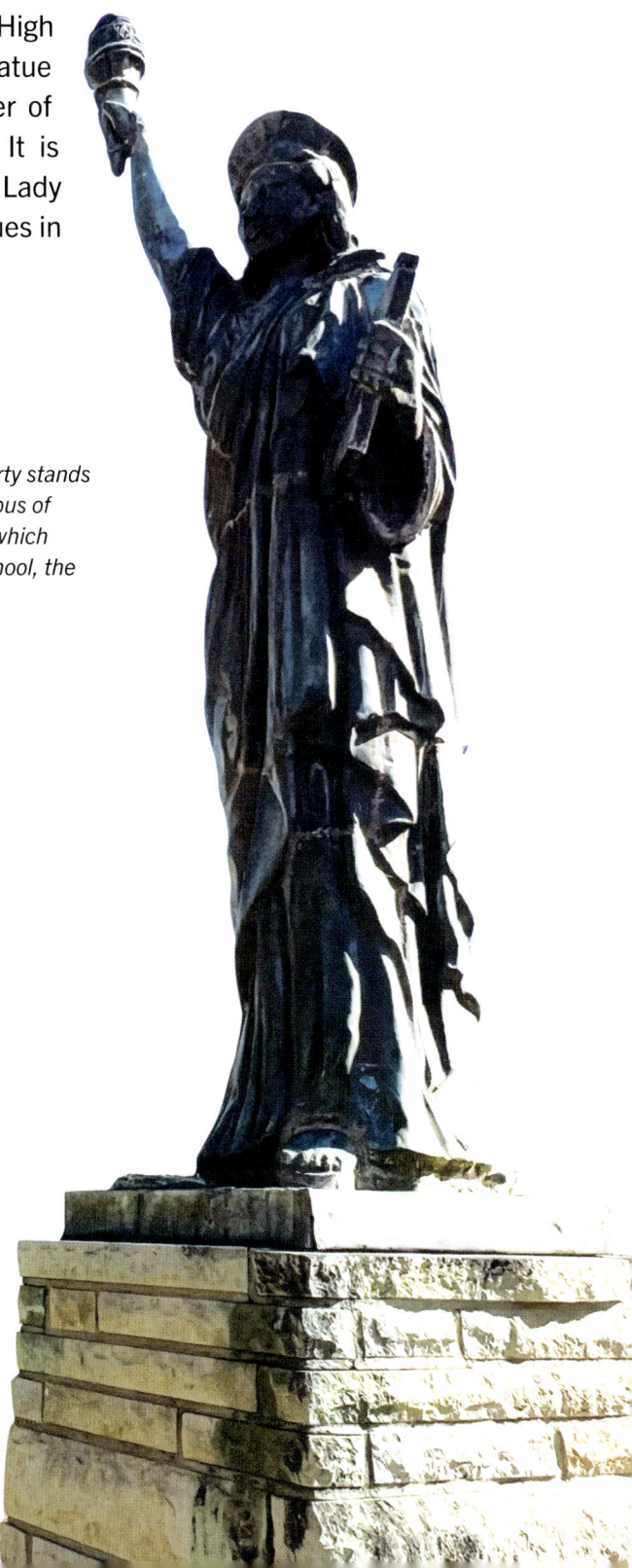

# BETTER IN BRONZE

**Why are cows, horses, foxes, and birds hanging out along Douglas Avenue?**

What is that mother pointing out to her child? And why is a young girl leading her horse along the sidewalk of downtown Wichita? Washington artist Georgia Gerber's bronze sculptures line both sides of the Douglas Avenue Streetscape. Thirty-one sculptures depict life-size animals and human figures, bringing a sense of whimsy to four blocks of the downtown corridor.

The permanent art installations are meant to encourage viewer interaction. It's not uncommon to see a hat or scarf added to the sculpture of *Barefoot Businessman* during the winter. Who decided he was cold and needed extra layers? One may never know.

During the summer, water emits from several of the sculptures to create movement and elicit the curiosity of passersby. Water trails from the statue of the child pushing a toy car. A bubbler of water rises from the sidewalk at another creation.

Other Gerber creations commissioned by the city include references to Wichita's historical moments. The Dockum Drugs store lunch counter sit-in depicts the Black student-led effort to end segregation, a victorious one that prompted other Rexall stores to change their policies. The artist's website reads, "Georgia is very pleased with the *Lunch Counter Sculpture* on many levels. She has always intended for her public art to be interactive, and is honored that the sculpture is used and

---

Wichita resident and philanthropist Dick DeVore saw Georgia Gerber's work in downtown Portland and approached the artist about creating sculptures for a similar project in Wichita.

*The Douglas Avenue Streetscape sculptures were installed in 2002.*

## DOUGLAS AVENUE SCULPTURES

**WHAT:** Public art

**WHERE:** Douglas Ave. between St. Francis Ave. and Main St.

**COST:** Free

**PRO TIP:** Look for free on-street parking downtown. Nearly all parking garages allow paid hourly or daily parking.

enjoyed, and especially that it has moved people and taken on meaning within the community."

Gerber's artwork is intended to engage the viewer's imagination and suggest a story. So, why is the businessman barefoot? And what is the mother trying to show her child? It's up to viewers to suggest the narrative.

# MAGNIFICIENT MURALS

**How can an artist's creativity and a whole lot of painting boost civic pride?**

If one is driving through the Douglas Design District, a three-mile stretch of road running east and west on Douglas Avenue, they're likely to notice vibrant murals. The corridor is home to oversized paintings by local artists as part of an initiative, Avenue Art Days, launched in 2015. Over 100 murals draw the eyes of passersby. Occasionally, people stop to have their photos taken before a mural of choice. The murals are often the draw for people who then visit restaurants and boutique stores.

The beautification project, also meant to boost civic pride, extends beyond using the sides of buildings as a canvas. Light poles, overpass columns, and crosswalks became a blank slate for artists. Why not paint the trashcans, too? Rolled out in multiple phases over the years, the bootstrapped project added colorful urban art to the streetscape.

While some of the murals' subject matter doesn't necessarily relate to the city or its location, other murals feature references to Wichita's history, industry,

---

## DOUGLAS DESIGN DISTRICT

**WHAT:** Murals

**WHERE:** Uptown to East of Oliver St.

**COST:** Free

**PRO TIP:** On a self-guided tour? Look up! Some installations, such as *Happy Triangles* by Sontia Levy-Mason, appear on the underside of a building's awning. The cemetery is also where many of the city's mayors are laid to rest.

---

Avenue Art Days was launched in 2015, allowing local artists to express their creativity in a mural format.

Colorblind Sunset by Baxter "Slim" Suber and Brady Scott was added to the north side of Lytton's Appliance Showroom near Douglas Ave. and Hillside St. in 2021. Scott's artwork typically combines Kansas flora and fauna.

and flag. For example, *Dear Wichita, Take Care and Dream Big* by Lindsey Kernodle & Friends features the Arkansas River, airplanes, and the downtown skyline. *Mead Crossing the Arkansas* by Philip Nellis shows one of the city's founders, J. R. Mead, crossing the river holding a Wichita flag. It was one of the first murals added to the collection.

In 2022, Avenue Art Days concluded its project with a final, 108th mural led by Heather Byers in collaboration with volunteers and other artists. *Looking to the Future* was inspired by Byers's appreciation for Kansas as an ideal place to live and work. Although the project has ended, mural hunters can still access the Avenue Art Days mobile app to reference a map that uses one's GPS location. Art admirers are encouraged to tag #avenueartdays when posting mural images to social media.

# THE ORIGINAL BUFFALO BILL

**How did a young man from Upstate New York become one of Wichita's founding fathers?**

Two men took on the name "Buffalo Bill." William Mathewson, a man who acquired a homestead near the Arkansas River in 1868, was the first to do so, followed by William Frederick "Buffalo Bill" Cody. Mathewson earned his nickname by hunting buffalo to feed starving settlers during the winter of 1860–1861.

A farmer's son, Mathewson worked in the lumber industry in Upstate New York and Pennsylvania before working for North West Fur Company in 1849. A frontiersman at heart, he also worked as an explorer, trader, hunter, and Indian scout employed by the United States government.

His pioneer days brought him to Wichita, where he established settlements and traded with Wichita Indians. Mathewson joined forces with James R. Mead, William Greiffenstein, and Jesse Chisholm in the Wichita area and Indian territory. He is

### HIGHLAND CEMETERY

**WHAT:** Grave

**WHERE:** Highland Cemetery, Section 1, Block 161, Grave 12

**COST:** Free

**PRO TIP:** Look for J.R. Mead's mausoleum near the cemetery's office. The cemetery is also where many of the city's mayors are laid to rest.

---

The Indian scout William Mathewson was referred to as "Long-Bearded Dangerous White Man" after defending his life in a battle with Kiowa Chief Satanta. Mathewson won the fight and Satanta's followers fled.

considered one of the city's founders for his many contributions. Not only did he become a civic leader, but he also served as president of the Wichita Savings Bank.

Mathewson died in his home, one of the first homes built in Wichita, at age 87 from complications due to asthma. The *Wichita Beacon* reported, "The extreme heat of the day probably aided in the cause of death. It had aggravated the case of asthma from which Mr. Mathewson has been suffering for some years and which had grown worse about 10 days ago." At his funeral, more than 600 people attended the Gill's Funeral Home ceremony where Judge Sluss said about Mathewson, "If he owed a debt, he paid it off. If he made an obligation, he kept it. If he had a friend, he stayed by him; he asked for nothing but gave all."

The city's founder is buried at Highland Cemetery. The former home of Mathewson, located at 1047 North Market Street, was listed for auction in the summer of 2022.

*The original "Buffalo Bill," William Mathewson, is buried at Wichita's Highland Cemetery next to his wives. His son's grave is also located nearby.*

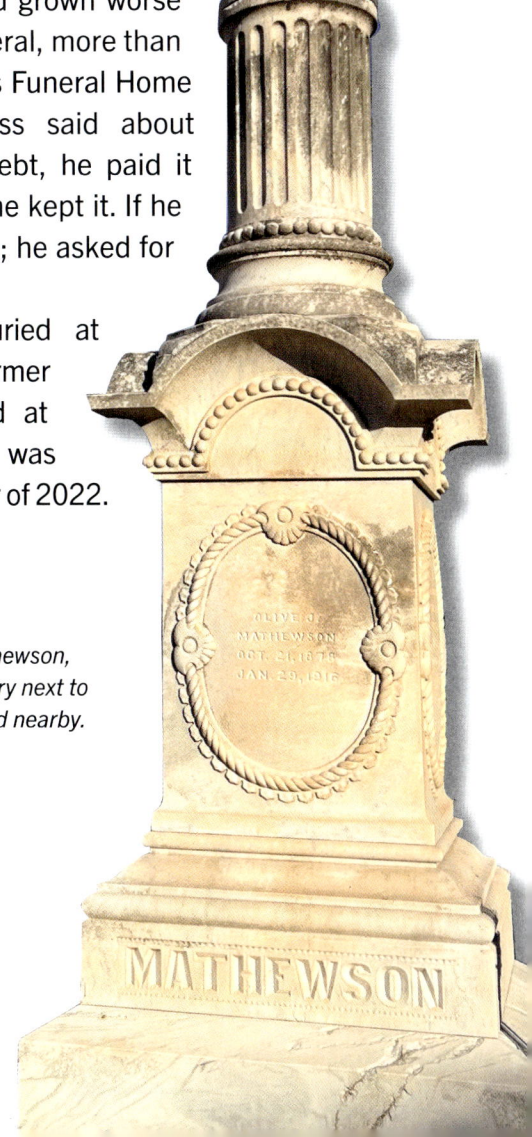

# TOTALLY TIKI

**Where in the city can one partake in merriment in maritime style?**

A scene from paradise awaits those who open a nondescript wooden door of a building in downtown Wichita. What lies behind it is something that you might not expect. Enter Lava & Tonic, a flagship tiki bar serving rum drinks and endless summer vibes year-round.

Patrons can expect to feel instantly transported to an island bar the moment they step inside. It's the kind of place where guests don't need to wear sunblock, but if they decided to visit while wearing a Hawaiian shirt and flip-flops, they'd fit right in.

The bar is dimly lit by colorful lights hanging overhead inside nautical-themed baskets. A black velvet painting of Elvis hangs on the wall near surfboards. Surf rock music conjures up thoughts of a sun-drenched day. Framed black and white photos of sailors and old maps adorn the walls inside of booth seating areas. Can you spot the mermaid swimming out of the wall?

---

### LAVA & TONIC

**WHAT:** Bar
**WHERE:** 1716 E Douglas Ave.
**COST:** Drinks $8–$15
**PRO TIP:** Ask about drink special pricing, including $7 happy hour cocktails.

---

Tiki bars became popular after World War II for their idyllic island living setting. Around the time of the 2008 recession, tiki bars flourished yet again.

*Bar seating is first come, first served. Table seating is available in two-hour blocks by reservation.*

    Behind the bar, almost 100 types of rum stand like soldiers at the ready. As the orders come in, the bartender carefully crafts each drink. Customers indulge in cocktails from tiki cups of Shark Bite or Teak 9 decorated with fruit garnish. Like a scene from a Caribbean paradise, Lava & Tonic gives city dwellers a place to unwind and relax.

# STRUMMING STEEL

**Is it true that the electric guitar debuted in Wichita?**

It's no secret that many of the city's residents have made history in their own way. What some people don't realize is that one man did something in Wichita that would change the music industry forever.

George Beauchamp, a musician, invented the electric guitar in 1931. The guitar's sound occurred when he placed a wired magnet next to the steel strings. The strings vibrated, and the sound amplified. He later gifted a guitar prototype to Wichita guitarist and band leader Gage Brewer. It was time for its official debut. On Halloween, 1932, Brewer was the first to give an electrical guitar performance, and it took place at Shadowland Dance Hall.

Prior to the performance, the band worked hard to create a buzz by encouraging the public to join in on the festivities. The October 1932 invitation read, "In the orchestra, we are at this time introducing two of the world's newest and most sensational instruments. A new invention which is startling the music world, making possible a combination of natural personal technique and electrical perfection."

Brewer's love of playing fretted instruments began at the age of 14. The young musician from Oklahoma was enamored with Hawaiian music. Eventually, he moved to Wichita in 1924 to begin a career in music, and went on to play at Shadowland with his eight-piece radio orchestra, Gage Brewer's Hawaiian Entertainers, regularly. The popular venue attracted people wanting to dance every night, except Sunday and Monday.

---

The city has a long list of guitarists who made their mark in music history, including native Wichitans Joe Walsh of the Eagles and Pat McJimsey, who toured with John Manning, Finnegan & Wood, Leon Russell, and Freddie King.

*The lap guitar on the chair is Brewer's Electric Hawaiian Guitar and Amplifier Set, 1936.*

A 1932–33 Ro-Pat-In "Electro" Guitar Spanish Model used by the Gage Brewer Orchestra, an example of the first commercial production electric guitar, is on display at Wichita-Sedgwick County Historical Museum. Other guitars on exhibit include the 1927 National Silver Guitar, Hawaiian Model, and Brewer's Electric Hawaiian Guitar and Amplifier Set, 1936.

# WICHITA-SEDGWICK COUNTY HISTORICAL MUSEUM

**WHAT:** Exhibit

**WHERE:** 204 S Main St.

**COST:** $5 adults, $2 children ages 6–12, free for children ages 6 and under

**PRO TIP:** Locally owned and operated Damm Music Center, 8945 W Central Ave., offers private guitar lessons for wannabe rockers.

# FRONTLINE FIGHTERS

**Where do you store a private collection of over a dozen military tanks?**

One man's hobby of collecting military tanks became the city's treasure when The House of Tank opened its doors to the public in 2020. Tanks ranging from the World War I–era M1917 to a more modern Leopard 1A5 are displayed for museumgoers to appreciate.

Where does one house over a dozen military tanks without drawing unwanted attention? Initially, the idea was to store them in a massive warehouse in the north end of Wichita. And then, at some point, the owner decided it was time to show off his private collection to others.

Inside, tanks of all sizes and capabilities are lined up like war soldiers. The warehouse is so quiet a pin could drop, and one wouldn't hear it. The warehouse lights shine down on tank guns like well-deserved spotlights as an American flag hangs on the wall in the background. The collection is not small by any means. Twenty-four tanks sit on display indoors, while three others rest outdoors near the museum's entrance.

The explanatory sign in front of each tank provides background information on its specifications and how it was used in a war. The bonus "cool fact" gives more insight into its tour of duty. For example, the Comet A34 Tank used by the British weighed 33 tons and reached a speed of 32 mph. The cruiser tank was the only one in the history of man to have a positive kill ratio against the Tiger I tank.

---

The indoor display left of the museum's entrance is filled with toy versions of the actual tanks on display.

*Two rows of tanks make up most of the collection in the larger of three rooms within the museum.*

## HOUSE OF TANK

**WHAT:** Museum

**WHERE:** 502 E 33rd St. N

**COST:** Requested donation of $5.

**PRO TIP:** Consider yourself a super fan of tanks? Plan to spend about an hour enjoying the museum.

But museum staff admit that one tank, in particular, interests history/movie enthusiasts. An M4A3E8 replica from the movie *Fury*, which starred actor Brad Pitt, garners attention. The United States used the M4 Sherman Tank, the most widely used tank by the Western Allies in World War II, because it was reliable and inexpensive to produce.

Museum attendees range from curious tourists and school groups on field trips to Wichita Rotary Club members and military veterans. Groups and classroom tours are always invited to visit the museum.

# HOME ON THE RANGE

### Where does the city's first house exist today?

The first house built in Wichita. the Munger House in 1868, is available to view at Old Cowtown Museum. Built for D. S. Munger, a cofounder of Wichita, the log cabin's plaster was made from the Arkansas River's sand, buffalo hair, and mussel shells. The windows and door hardware were freighted from Emporia.

The Wichita leader occupied the house with his wife and daughter. Ms. Mary E. Munger Watson told the *Wichita Eagle* newspaper that her father built the house himself. "In those days, where most of the city of Wichita now is, was then nothing but prairie, and there wasn't a tree between the Little Arkansas River and Chisholm Creek."

Munger's two-story house was originally constructed north of Ninth Street and Waco Avenue and served many purposes over the years. It was his family's personal home, and it also served as a makeshift boarding house, hospital, and post office. As the city's second postmaster, Munger often carried letters in his hat. On occasion, church services took place upstairs in the home, so he also was referred to as Father Munger by community members.

### OLD COWTOWN MUSEUM

**WHAT:** House

**WHERE:** 1865 Museum Blvd.

**COST:** $9 for adults, $8 for seniors (62+), $7 for youth 12–17, $6 for kids 5–11, free for kids 4 and under

**PRO TIP:** Walk on the sagging wood floor inside the home to get a close look at the kitchen. When the gas lamp is lit, the place transforms visitors to an earlier time in the city's history.

Today, Munger Post Office at 1314 N Oliver St. displays a photo on the wall of D. S. Munger and the city's first post office.

*The Munger House was listed on the National Register of Historic Places in 1982. It is considered to be the first settlement property in Wichita.*

   In 1874, the city's first banker, W. C. Woodman, purchased the home. He chose to build a Victorian house around it. The original Munger House was discovered when the "Lakeside Mansion" was demolished in the 1940s. Eventually, the home was purchased by the Eunice Sterling Chapter of the Daughters of the American Revolution and given to Historic Wichita, Inc. in 1952. The house was relocated to the Old Cowtown Museum's grounds, where it was restored.

# TINY TOWNS

**What if it was possible to flash back to 1950s Kansas in the blink of an eye?**

*Kansas in Miniature* is unlike anything one has probably seen before, and if they are a native Kansan, it's a rite-of-passage experience. The Exploration Place exhibit brings small-town Kansas to life, including many of its notable landmarks.

The animated diorama of 1950s Kansas includes 125 scale-model buildings, 200 period vehicles, 1,000 people, and more than 3,000 pieces of landscape. The sights and sounds of a full day from sun-up to after dark make the sensory experience an unforgettable one. The tiny figure of a man waves from the Nickerson water tower. With the push of a button, a train winds its way through the exhibit, passing farmers at work in the fields and children running to the one-room schoolhouse. At the drive-in theatre, vintage cars are parked with passengers watching a live motion picture. Running water flows through rivers and ponds. Carnival rides, including an intricate carousel, stay in motion with lights that illuminate the night scene. Natural features like Mushroom Rock in Ellsworth County and part of the Gypsum Hills represent the southern landforms, while prairie scenes showcase the vastness of the Sunflower State.

The fan-favorite exhibit at the museum is always evolving, thanks to the assistance of museum staff. Surprises await each time guests visit, especially during special events. When the museum hosted a temporary dinosaur exhibit, small-scale T-Rex and Pterodactyl figurines were positioned through the streets

---

Technicians crawl under the massive table that supports the scaled-down version of the Kansas diorama when they need to work on its wires, hydraulics, and gears. The lights are computer-controlled and set to timers.

*An original exhibit of Exploration Place, Kansas in Miniature, opened with the museum in 2000. The diorama includes Wichita buildings such as the first NuWay restaurant, and Planeview, a community established after World War II to house defense workers.*

## EXPLORATION PLACE

**WHAT:** Exhibit

**WHERE:** 300 N McLean Blvd.

**COST:** $12 for adults, $10 for seniors, $10 for kids Ages 3–11, free for kids ages 2 and under

**PRO TIP:** To learn more about Kansas, tour the permanent exhibit *Explore Kansas* to drive a combine, step into an EF1 tornado, and learn about the Sunflower State's geology and water sources.

and farms. It's not uncommon to see Christmas trees or pumpkins as a part of the scenery during the holidays. And some figurines are what one would least expect—where is Bigfoot?

Visitors touring *Kansas in Miniature* are encouraged to grab a complimentary map to help them identify the buildings and landmarks.

# MOVIE LEGEND

**Which one-time Wichita resident won an Academy Award and appeared on a United States postage stamp?**

She was born to be a star. Hattie McDaniel was the first Black actor to receive an Academy Award. She was recognized with the Best Supporting Actress award for her performance as Mammy in the 1939 film *Gone With the Wind*. A historical marker showcasing her life and career is located near her childhood home near Ninth Street and Waco Avenue. The youngest of 13 children, she was born in Wichita on June 10, 1895.

During McDaniel's career, she worked to change people's opinions of African American actors. She chose roles playing independent characters, and she refused to speak with a dialect that many African American actors were forced to use at the time. The Oscar-winning actress appeared in 37 movies and became the star of *The Beulah Show*, a radio show that was later televised. As fate would have it, her performance on the show was her last. McDaniel died from breast cancer at age 57 on October 26, 1952. She is laid to rest in the Garden of Legends at Angelus Rosedale Cemetery in Los Angeles, California.

---

**HATTIE MCDANIEL BIRTHPLACE**

**WHAT:** Historical marker

**WHERE:** 925 N Wichita St.

**COST:** Free

**PRO TIP:** The marker is viewable from a walking and bike path east of Waco Ave., between 8th and 9th sts. On-street parking is available.

---

The United States Postal Service issued a 39-cent commemorative stamp in 2006 featuring Hattie McDaniel, the 29th stamp in the Black Heritage Series.

*A historical marker sits in front of Hattie McDaniel's childhood home. The Orpheum Theatre debuted the film* Gone With the Wind, *featuring the actress, in 1940.*

At the 2021 dedication of the historical marker in Wichita, Denise Sherman, executive director of The Kansas African American Museum, spoke about McDaniel's contributions to the performing arts. The actress and singer is also recognized in the museum's Trailblazers Hall of Fame.

69

# DARING DESIGN

**What's the story behind the Wichita State University campus building that looks dramatically different from the others?**

Corbin Education Center on the north end of Wichita State University's (WSU) campus was designed by acclaimed architect Frank Lloyd Wright. Dedicated in 1964, it was one of his last projects before his death in 1959. Upon his death, the university had not received the final blueprints from the architect, but the 10-year project continued.

His visionary design incorporated two buildings joined by an esplanade with a water fountain feature running down its center. A 50-foot entrance connects the administrative building to the classroom building. Ceiling-high windows give faculty and students a view of the outdoors, a design trait of Wright's projects.

The architect's unique style adds to other areas of the complex. The 40,000-square-foot space includes sheltered outdoor balconies, terraces, and shaded areas with tables. Following Wright's Prairie Style, his design choices use horizontal lines, and the interior walls are minimized to emphasize

## CORBIN EDUCATION CENTER

**WHAT:** Building

**WHERE:** 21st St. and Yale St.

**COST:** Free

**PRO TIP:** A second design by Frank Lloyd Wright, Allen House, is located at 255 N Roosevelt St. Guided tours of the 1918 home are available.

The building was named in honor of former university president Harry F. Corbin Jr., who also was responsible for constructing the arena on campus.

*A skylight adorns the top of each of the two buildings at Corbin Education Center, a structure that is a protected historical site.*

openness. Intentionally, the buildings and surrounding landscape become one. It was reported that his wife, Olgivanna, influenced the building's exterior color scheme of pink, brown, orange, and aqua blue.

At the building's dedication ceremony in 1964, Wright's wife said, "I have been at the dedication of several of the buildings he designed late in life, and I never cease to be amazed at the outstanding difference of every one of them." Former WSU president Corbin did not attend the event because of a schedule conflict.

# CONFIDENTIAL COCKTAILS

**What lies behind the wooden door in the basement of a historic hotel?**

Harry Dockum opened three downtown drugstores within blocks of one another after he arrived in Wichita in 1899. He probably never envisioned a speakeasy-style bar occupying part of the same building, with a history dating to 1926.

Kansas enacted prohibition in 1881, making it illegal to make or sell alcohol. Speakeasies opened in secret den-like places in the state to provide a place where customers could gather and enjoy a drink. Once referred to as "soft drink places," speakeasy owners obtained liquor secretly and served patrons at night. It was written in the *Western Methodist* newspaper in 1890, "This is precisely the way it is done in Wichita. But, then, Wichita presents the exception and not the rule under Prohibition."

Fast forward to today's Dockum bar: its design reflects a secret-like space to sip on cocktails, just as patrons did decades ago. The low-light drinking establishment is the meeting space for friends sitting on leather couches or at bar tables, drinking cocktails, and listening to jazz favorites. Candles flicker from wall sconces. The bartender mixes libations using fresh-squeezed juices, house-made bitters, and liquor.

---

Dockum Drugs store was the site of a lunch counter sit-in in the summer of 1958. The store had an unwritten policy of denying seated service to Black people. The nonviolent protest resulted in service for Black patrons at other Rexall stores across the state.

*The bartenders are referred to as pharmacists, a term consistent with the history of a portion of the building that once served as a drugstore.*

## DOCKUM

**WHAT:** Bar

**WHERE:** 104 S Broadway St.

**COST:** Cocktails $12–$18

**PRO TIP:** Follow the signs with the pharmacy logo through the Ambassador Hotel to locate the underground speakeasy. Knock on the door to let the staff know of your arrival at the reserved time.

Reservations to Dockum are encouraged, although seats at the bar are first-come, first-served. The basement bar is open during evening hours and can accommodate private parties inside the Dispensary Vault. Its bar menu includes drinks with names like the Smoking Gun and Dizzy Dame.

# MADE IN WICHITA

**Why did an entrepreneur think he could make a better car than Henry Ford?**

John Jones was different from the average Iowa teenager. He was an entrepreneur who purchased old items, including automobiles, to repair or rebuild for sale. In 1910, he bought used cars and shipped them back to Wichita. Later, he traveled to Kansas City to secure the Ford franchise for Wichita and 17 Kansas counties. The Jones Auto Exchange opened in 1910, and he and his partner designed and built the Jones Six car. The car, designed and built from 1915 to 1921, was unique because it was a six-cylinder car when four-cylinder vehicles were standard.

Today, an original Jones Six car sits on exhibit at the Wichita-Sedgwick County Historical Museum in a replicated garage under workshop lights. The room smells like greasy car parts—a vintage gasoline tank towers in the corner. Mechanics' tools from an earlier time are strewn about as if workers abandoned them before returning home at the end of the work day.

Wichita workers carefully produced each car, from its steel body to the wood wheels. The Jones Six was manufactured like a kit car; its exterior was hand-painted. The museum's exhibit reads, "Jones painters prided themselves on being able to match any colors requested (pink and yellow were especially popular)." On April 29, 1915, an advertisement by the Jones Motor Car Company appeared in the *Wichita Eagle*, announcing a chance for readers to enter a giveaway to "get this wonderful car without investing a dollar." Participants earned points for submitting the names of potential car buyers. If they bought a car, participants

---

The museum housing the car once served as the city building. Referred to as the Palace of the Plains, it was completed in 1892.

*This Jones Six car, purchased from Wichitan Bud Redmond in 1966, was placed inside the museum's fourth-story window using a crane on April 23, 1979. It remains on display on the museum's fourth floor.*

## WICHITA-SEDGWICK COUNTY HISTORICAL MUSEUM

**WHAT:** Jones Six car

**WHERE:** 204 S Main St.

**COST:** $5 for adults, $2 for children ages 6–12, free for children ages 6 and under

**PRO TIP:** Tour *The Spirit of Wichita* exhibit to understand the scope of entrepreneurship that dominated the city from 1912–1939.

earned more points. The first prize went to the person who earned the most points.

Jones's company produced an estimated 3,000 cars and trucks in Wichita. After a fire burned down the Jones Motor Company in 1920, the company went out of business. Four Jones Six cars exist today.

75

# ALLEY ART

**Why are massive metal spiders crawling up the side of a downtown building?**

How did an underutilized alley between two downtown buildings become a public art destination?

A grant from the Knight Foundation and the Wichita Community Foundation made it possible to bring the Gallery Alley concept to life in 2017. The alley continues to evolve, but always includes unique public art pieces on display for downtowngoers to appreciate. It's where metal spiders crawl on a building's facade, and ceramic flowers appear to grow from a brick wall.

The permanent art exhibit serves as a "playground for the senses" to highlight local artists' work. In 2022, a second metal spider by artist Mike Miller was added on the side of one of the alley's neighboring buildings.

Envision, a local nonprofit that provides opportunities to people who are blind or visually impaired, partnered with Downtown Wichita to give the alley a facelift in 2021. The latest updates include intercessory pieces, allowing

### GALLERY ALLEY

**WHAT:** Public art

**WHERE:** 616 E Douglas Ave.

**COST:** Free

**PRO TIP:** Walk north down the alley until it ends and then west along the back alley until you see Old Mill Tasty Shop's backdoor mural painted by award-winning artist Ande Hall, *Les Grandes Bresses*.

---

Shops at Gallery Alley are home to ground-floor retail stores. The buildings on both sides of the brick-paved alley date back to the city's founding.

*Multisensory art installations provide a tactile experience for art lovers who walk the alley.*

people with reduced vision to experience art through touch. The public art project earned recognition with a Downtown Achievement of Excellence award from the International Downtown Association.

# GRAIN ELEVATOR GALLERY

**What Guinness World Record was set by an artist in 2020?**

*El Sueno Original*, also known as *The Original Dream*, is the largest mural in the world painted by a single artist. The mural is shown on the side of the Beachner Grain Elevator near 21st and Broadway streets. The brightly colored street art was spearheaded by Armando Minjarez, a local artist and the director of the Horizontes Project.

Considerable thought and research by the Horizontes Project was done before a single drop of paint was added to the grain elevator's exterior. Minjarez surveyed residents and business owners about their history in the north-end neighborhood. Later, a street artist from Colombia, GLeo, was hired to paint the 50,000-square-foot mural that connects two distinct north areas: historically Black and Latinx neighborhoods. The record-breaking project used over 600 gallons of paint, applied with rollers and brushes.

The Latin American urban artist painted people of color with a woman in the center looking toward the horizon. According to Horizontes Project, GLeo's painting "demonstrates the audacity of solidarity among people of color (and beyond) to reimagine, in practice, how to live and work with one another, expanding the circle of human connection."

The artist, who started painting street art early on, often added sea creatures to murals in her neighborhood. Today, her style usually includes yellow-eyed masks, a trademark of

---

*The Original Dream*'s colors appear to glow during a sunrise, which is visible from nearby Interstate 135.

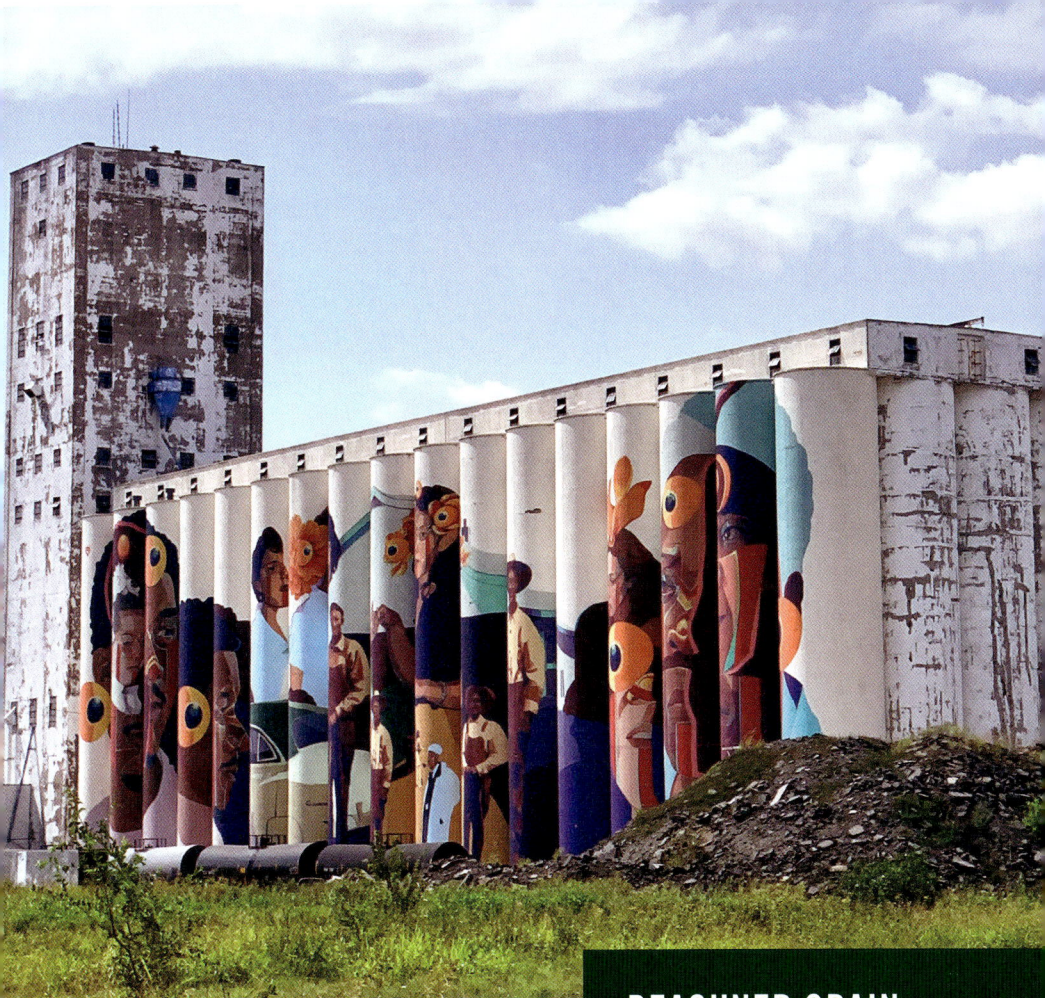

*The grain elevator is located in an industrial area west of I-135 and adjacent to train tracks. The neighborhood is home to over 20 murals by various artists.*

her paintings. In an interview with SupportStreetArt.com, she said, "they (yellow-eyed masks) are a constant element that is a symbol of the cycle and the infinite."

## BEACHNER GRAIN ELEVATOR

**WHAT:** Mural

**WHERE:** 519 E 20th St. N

**COST:** Free

**PRO TIP:** To see more examples of street art near *The Original Dream*, visit horizontes-project.com.

# MADWOMAN MAKES MISCHIEF

**What would drive a woman to destroy a bar?**

It was 7 p.m. on December 27, 1900, and the Carey Hotel's bar was bustling with activity. Carry A. Nation, a women-led Temperance Movement member, entered the bar and began her saloon-wrecking brigade. Her mission? To keep people from selling and consuming alcoholic beverages. Her efforts predated the start of the nationwide Prohibition Era in 1920, when the United States Constitution prohibited "the manufacture, sale, or transportation of intoxicating liquors."

The cherrywood bar with brass rail was adorned with cut-glass decanters, the ideal targets for her cane. But a life-size painting on the wall above the bar infuriated the already upset, six-foot, 180-pound woman. In an instant, she hurled a rock at *Cleopatra at the Bath*, a $300 painting by Wichita-based artist John Noble that hung over the bar. According to *The Wichita Reader: A Collection of Writing About a Prairie City*, she exclaimed, "It's disgraceful!

### EATON PLACE

**WHAT:** Statue

**WHERE:** 517 E Douglas Ave.

**COST:** Free

**PRO TIP:** The building is registered on the National Register of Historic Places. Walk inside Eaton Place to view its original architecture and tile flooring.

---

Nation resided in Medicine Lodge, Kansas, from 1890 until the early 1900s. The Carry A. Nation Home Museum is open for tours. Inside, visitors can view memorabilia from her crusade.

You're insulting your mother by having her form stripped naked and hung up in a place where it is not even decent for a woman to be shown she has her clothes on!"

Nation was jailed many times, along with several opinionated women who often accompanied her to saloons. Eventually, she returned to the Carey Hotel, where she was stopped by police and hauled away to jail again. A reporter, who passed the story on the wire to newspapers, suggested a hatchet would make a better weapon for Carry, so she upgraded her weapon of choice. She continued to make her opinions known by editing the newsletters *The Smasher's Mail, The Hatchet,* and *The Home Defender*, and she earned money as a temperance lecturer.

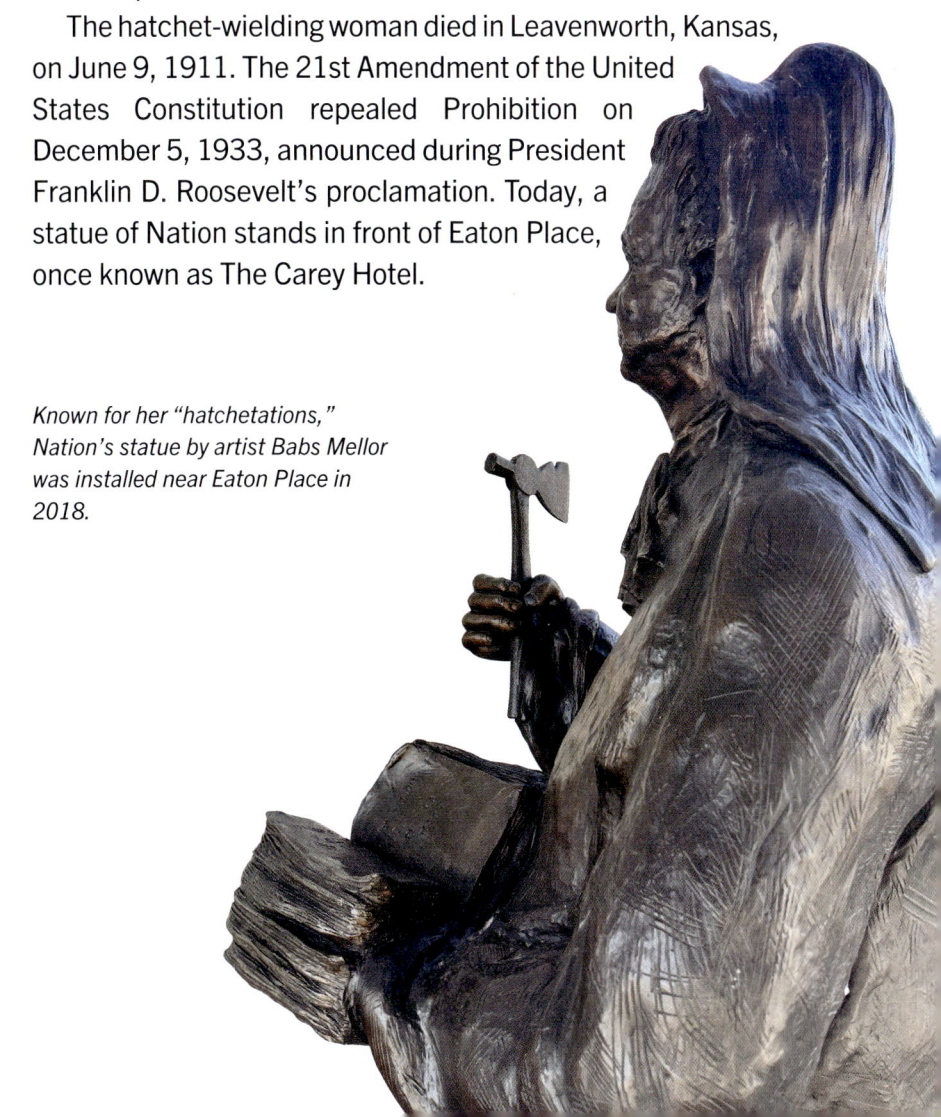

The hatchet-wielding woman died in Leavenworth, Kansas, on June 9, 1911. The 21st Amendment of the United States Constitution repealed Prohibition on December 5, 1933, announced during President Franklin D. Roosevelt's proclamation. Today, a statue of Nation stands in front of Eaton Place, once known as The Carey Hotel.

*Known for her "hatchetations," Nation's statue by artist Babs Mellor was installed near Eaton Place in 2018.*

# MERRY-GO-ROUND MEMORIES

**What became of the carousel from Joyland amusement park?**

Ask most Wichita natives about their fondest childhood memories, and they will probably tell you about Joyland. The long-gone amusement park was a go-to attraction for families. For 59 years, the carousel's pipe organ was the musical backdrop of the park.

While the entertainment destination didn't survive, its carousel did. Joyland's owner donated the carousel to Botanica in 2014, 10 years after the amusement park closed its doors. The Khicha Carousel is fully operational today, providing new memories for future generations.

An artist incorporated botanical references into the carousel's restored graphics while maintaining the look that people remember. Over 30 original horses and chariots were restored to their splendor. A handmade organ, Midget Monster, plays upbeat music like the original Wurlitzer organ, the Mammoth Monster, did at Joyland years ago.

Visitors to the 9,000-square-foot carousel's pavilion can purchase ride tokens at a self-pay kiosk. A ride attendant is

---

It took four years to bring the old carousel back to life, and each pony took 75 to 200 hours to restore due to extensive damage and multiple layers of paint.

available to answer questions. The carousel operates year-round inside an enclosed pavilion Monday through Saturday, 10 a.m. to 4 p.m.

## BOTANICA WICHITA

**WHAT:** Carousel

**WHERE:** 701 Amidon St.

**COST:** $10 for adults, $8 for seniors/youth/military, free for children 2 and under

**PRO TIP:** Miss the smell of cotton candy or popcorn from the early days of Joyland? A concession stand sells snacks in the room adjacent to the carousel.

# SPIRITS AMONG US

**How does one explain the unexplainable?**

The Kansas Aviation Museum was Wichita's original municipal airport. Constructed in the 1930s, the airport served as a midpoint for cross-country travelers. During the 1940s, it was one of the busiest airports in the nation, with an incoming plane landing or departing every 90 seconds. The building is said to be alive with paranormal activity, and it hosts ghost tours for interested visitors on occasion.

According to Terri Pratt of Spirit Hunters Paranormal Society (SHPS), the investigative team began detecting paranormal activity at Kansas Aviation Museum in 2017. They work for free. Using structured light sensor (SLS) cameras, K2 electromagnetic field meters, dousing rods, and temperature gauges, they seek to measure paranormal activity in the building.

The Engine Room containing Lloyd Stearman's 1960 Mercedes-Benz is busy with activity. SHPS members report they often detect him sitting in the car with someone in the passenger seat, and the K2 meter picks up a voice responding to them. Once, a flashlight turned on and off upon command.

In another museum area that houses a red and white 1931 Stearman Model 4D plane, a pilot named Duke is said to flirt with women who visit the room. When female voices ask questions, the K2 meter spikes with red notifications, and in another room dedicated to exhibits for children, SHPS has picked up voices of kids singing and laughing. SHPS members reported that a child's spirit in the next room makes the toy plane hanging from

---

Spirit Hunters Paranormal Society is a volunteer organization based in Wichita that investigates historical homes and buildings using professional equipment.

*Lloyd Stearman and his wife, Ethyl, used the 1960 Mercedes-Benz to tour Europe before shipping it to the United States. The car, which still runs, was donated to the museum in 2010 by the Stearmans' daughter, Marilyn.*

the ceiling turn on command, spinning forward and then in reverse.

These incidents of paranormal activity are part of a longer list of detections registered by SHPS. The building is considered an active paranormal space, from objects moving on their own in the museum's offices to a child's handprint appearing on a window.

## KANSAS AVIATION MUSEUM

**WHAT:** Paranormal activity

**WHERE:** 3350 S George Washington Blvd.

**COST:** Tickets $30

**PRO TIP:** Follow the museum's Facebook page to learn about upcoming paranormal investigation events.

# BASEBALL BRILLIANCE

**What could people accomplish in life if they bet on themselves?**

Does baseball phenom Jackie Robinson have a direct connection to Wichita? Not necessarily, but what he accomplished as an athlete and in baseball during his career inspires young players at League 42's ballfields. A life-size bronze sculpture of Robinson, created by Wichita artist John Parsons, was unveiled in 2021 at Jackie Robinson Pavilion in McAdams Park. It rests on a base in the shape of a baseball diamond.

League 42 was named in honor of Robinson, the first African American to break the color barrier in Major League Baseball while playing for the Brooklyn Dodgers in 1947. Robinson's uniform number was 42. The Wichita nonprofit consists primarily of urban youth ages 5 through 14 and prides itself on making the sport accessible, thanks to an affordable registration fee that includes a uniform and equipment.

Robinson's legacy lives on at the park. League 42's founder, Bob Lutz, told the *Wichita Eagle* in 2021, "He had great passion. He

## LEAGUE 42

**WHAT:** Sculpture

**WHERE:** McAdams Park near baseball fields

**COST:** Free

**PRO TIP:** Access League 42's Facebook page to view event information and learn how to donate to the nonprofit organization.

---

League 42's indoor facility across the street is used for baseball training and an after-school tutoring program. The sculpture faces the building, and the crosswalk is shaped like a baseball bat.

*Jackie Robinson's uniform number, 42, serves as the namesake for League 42. The artist of the bronze sculpture, John Parsons, also created the sculpture,* Fighting Bucks*, located at WaterWalk Wichita.*

had great vision, And he knew he wanted to be special. Those are all things we want to instill in our kids to study Jackie Robinson and get to know what he was about. I think our kids take pride in Jackie Robinson. We want the lessons that he taught to be lessons that they deem valuable."

Was there anything the baseball player couldn't do? Robinson made headlines as a baseball player and led the Pacific Coast Conference in scoring twice in basketball, became the NCAA champion in 1940 in the broad jump, and achieved All-American status in football. Robinson once said, "Life is not a spectator sport. If you're going to spend your whole life in the grandstand just watching what goes on, in my opinion, you're wasting your life." League 42 allows Wichita youth to get in the game and thrive.

# SOMEWHERE OVER THE RAINBOW

**Why was a bridge in the city considered "one of the finest in the Southwest" when it was built?**

The John Mack Bridge is notable for its unique design and impressive construction. Dedicated on July 22, 1931, the bridge is a finalist for the 8 Wonders of Kansas Architecture because it is the longest remaining James Barney Marsh Rainbow Bridge in Kansas and the second-longest in the United States. It spans the Big Arkansas River and remains a high-traffic, two-lane road in south Wichita.

James Barney Marsh, "the father of good Kansas roads," patented the "rainbow arch" design in 1911. It uses multiple concrete spans, a concept that was used to design 76 bridges in Kansas between 1917 and 1940. Eleven bridges, including the John Mack Bridge, are listed in the National Register of Historic Places. Its design allows for the reinforced concrete's expansion and contraction despite varying temperatures and moisture conditions.

So who was John C. Mack, and why was the bridge named after him? He was a man who wore many hats throughout his career. He came to Kansas in 1887 and taught school in Hesston and Newton. He became a newspaper manager, postmaster, and Kansas senator who served on the State Highway Commission and also was known as "the father of good Kansas roads."

---

The cost of the bridge and paved areas leading to it totaled $191,000 in 1931. Sixty years later, a community effort to "Save the John Mack Bridge" succeeded.

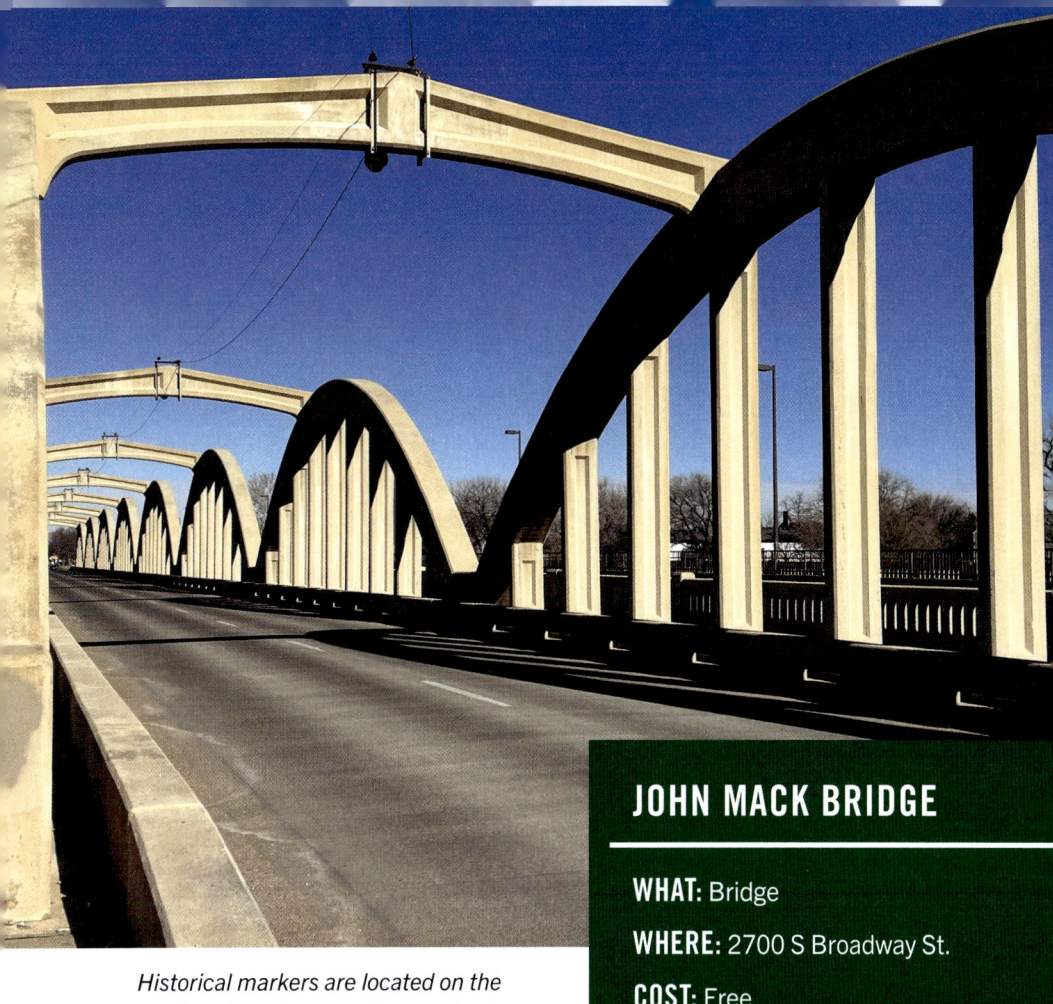

*Historical markers are located on the north and south ends of the bridge. It was also referred to as the South Lawrence Street Bridge in early documents.*

### JOHN MACK BRIDGE

**WHAT:** Bridge

**WHERE:** 2700 S Broadway St.

**COST:** Free

**PRO TIP:** Walk to the bridge's north or south end to view its identical historical markers.

Unfortunately, Mack succumbed to complications from kidney surgery and died at home on January 29, 1930, so he was absent for the bridge's dedication ceremony. However, his wife was introduced to the crowd attending the celebration.

Renovations to preserve the bridge's functionality and design were completed in 1997.

# TWISTED TREE LIMBS

**What could you create by bending branches into something else?**

*Oh, Give Me A Home* by artist Patrick Dougherty may resemble small buildings at first glance. Or perhaps they are small dwellings. On closer inspection, visitors to the Mark Arts outdoor sculpture garden will realize that Dougherty's public artwork consists of walls made from natural materials.

The Oklahoma-born artist began using his carpentry skills and love of nature to craft his first work in the early 1980s. Now, his environmental works are seen worldwide. The self-proclaimed "sapling sculptor" says that "a good sculpture is one that creates lots of personal associations." To date, the artist has imagined and created over 300 large-scale works.

Dougherty used dogwood, elm, and willow tree limbs gathered locally for the Mark Arts installation to create cylindrical structures. Each stick was gathered, grouped, and then shaped in a sweeping direction to create the illusion of movement. At 12 feet tall, *Oh, Give Me A Home* towers over onlookers. Adults walk through the sculpture

## MARK ARTS

**WHAT:** Sculpture

**WHERE:** 1307 N Rock Rd.

**COST:** Free to tour outdoors

**PRO TIP:** Contact the museum to request a Stickwork tour for a small group.

---

Mark Arts teachers provide sculpture classes for beginners and experienced artists. Students do not have to be museum members to participate.

Oh, Give Me A Home *is one of the latest installations in the Mark Arts Sculpture Garden, consisting of over a dozen works of art.*

to exit on the opposite side while children gleefully lead the way. Each structure's large windows provide visitors with views of a perfectly framed sky.

The public art display will remain in place for at least two years from its installment in May 2022. Then, the museum staff will inspect the piece to ensure it remains structurally sound.

# MOMENT IN TIME

**Why did a wealthy businessman purchase an empty building in the center of the city?**

One of the most picturesque places in the city comes with a building with a survival story all its own. Constructed as University Hall for Garfield University in 1888, the building is now known as Davis Administration Building at Friends University. The building held more floor space under one roof than any other educational facility west of the Mississippi. Even today, its impressive clock tower and Romanesque-style design remain an eye-catching addition to the city's downtown skyline and the center of the Friends University campus.

When Wichita's economic bubble burst and property values decreased, a mortgage of $65,000 was placed on the building and its grounds, and eventually, Garfield University closed. For five years, the once-attractive building sat boarded up, empty, and for sale. Finally, a wealthy Quaker businessman, James M. Davis, bought the building for $50,000 and donated it to the Society of Friends (Quakers).

In the *Wichita Eagle* on January 18, 1923, it was reported that Davis realized the building's potential when "he stood in the middle of an uninhabited prairie, tore off the boards from a basement window,

## DAVIS ADMINISTRATION BUILDING

**WHAT:** Architecture

**WHERE:** 2100 W University Ave.

**COST:** Free

**PRO TIP:** Tour the exterior of the Davis Administration Building.

---

The clock tower's cherrywood pendulum swings 40 times in a minute. During humid weather it slows down, and during dry weather it becomes lighter and speeds up.

*A Wichita landmark, the Davis Administration Building on the Friends University campus, was built from 1886–1888 and named for President James A. Garvey.*

went inside and roamed about . . . Friends University now is a well-established institution, and prosperous as college prosperity goes." Eventually, the building was renamed Davis Administration Building in 1923 in honor of Davis and his wife, Anna.

Over 50 years later, the brick and stone building was added to the National Register of Historic Places, properly recognizing its elaborate design. The building's distinctive architecture includes a 148-foot-tall clock tower and a stained glass rose window on its west side. Its Alumni Auditorium is used for fine arts performances and weekly chapel ceremonies.

# TIRELESSLY STANDING

**Did you spot the Muffler Man statue holding the tire?**

Roadside attractions don't get much better than the Muffler Man at Brown's Tire and Custom Wheel Center in south Wichita. He is holding a tire in his right hand; the oversized statue is so large that the tire he is holding looks small in comparison. You can't miss him. He is dressed in blue denim jeans and a bright red shirt.

Why would a tire store install a massive fiberglass statue in front of it? The tradition started in the 1960s by a California fiberglass company for gas station chains, according to the website Roadside America. Also referred to as American Giants, the roadside guys were created as a marketing strategy to draw attention to a business in a way neon signs could not. During the 1950s, many companies had neon signs, but not all of them had a 18- to 25-foot-tall Muffler Man statue. The hands of the figure were molded to hold an item, and it was often a muffler or tire. However, other versions of the two-story giants were created, including female versions.

Today, fewer than 200 of these statues exist, but one company is on a mission to help the giants live on. The International Fiberglass Company helps business owners

> **BROWN'S TIRE AND CUSTOM WHEEL CENTER**
>
> **WHAT:** Fiberglass statue
>
> **WHERE:** 4203 S Broadway St.
>
> **COST:** Free
>
> **PRO TIP:** Drive a couple blocks north of the tire store to catch a glimpse of an oversized lighthouse statue on the east side of Broadway St.

Less than 200 of the roadside Muffler Man statues exist today. A 19-foot statue of a miner holding a pickaxe is on display on US Route 66 in Galena, Kansas.

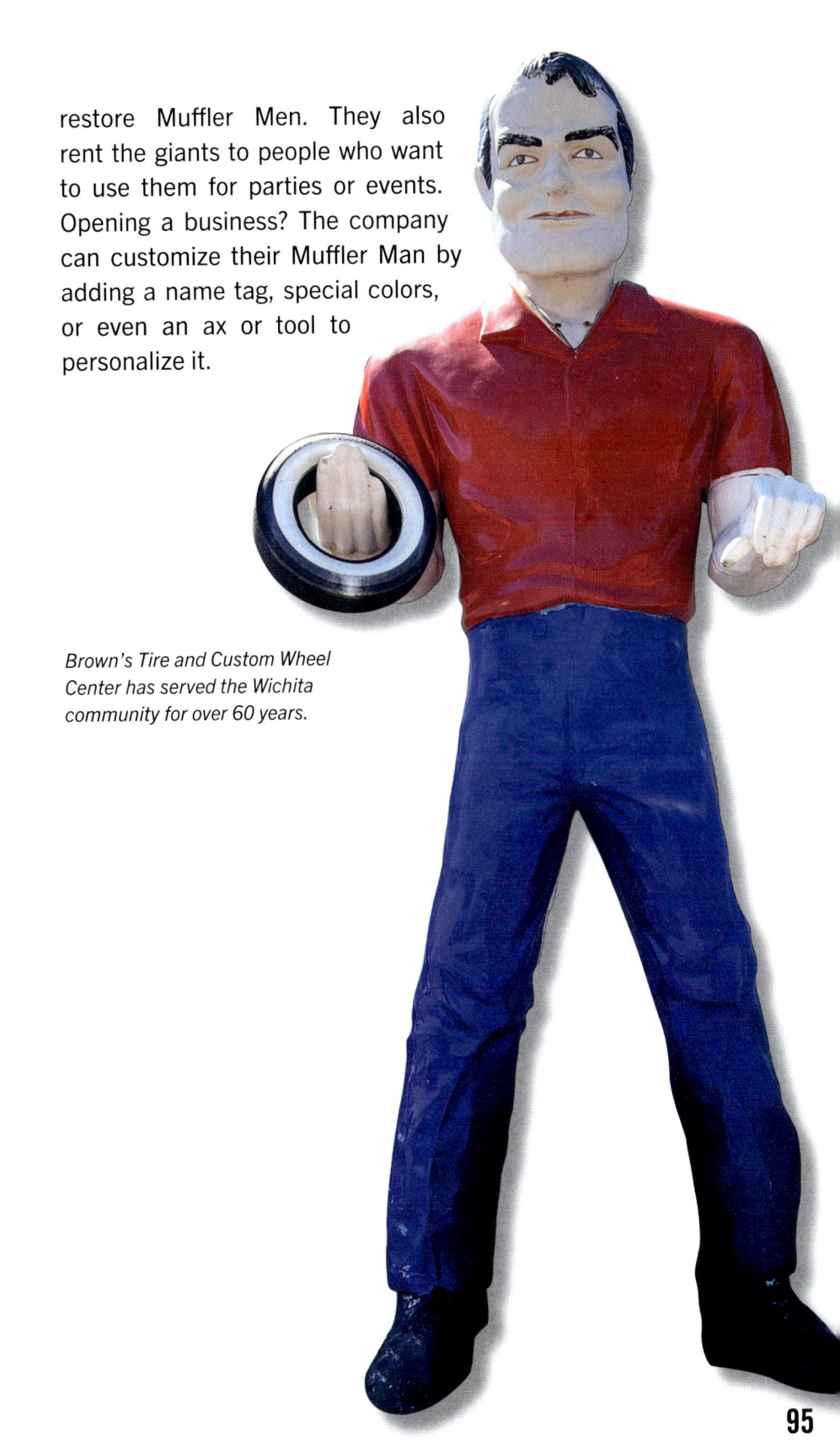

restore Muffler Men. They also rent the giants to people who want to use them for parties or events. Opening a business? The company can customize their Muffler Man by adding a name tag, special colors, or even an ax or tool to personalize it.

*Brown's Tire and Custom Wheel Center has served the Wichita community for over 60 years.*

# COFFIN CURIOSITY

**How did mummy coffins end up in Wichita, and what's their connection to the American Civil War?**

Have you ever looked upon a mummified body or looked inside its coffin? At the Museum of World Treasures, visitors can visit the *Ancient Egypt* exhibit and come face-to-face with two 3,000-year-old female mummies, coffins, and artifacts of the historical period.

The museum's coffins belonged to Tarutu, a deceased chanter who sang in the Temple of Amun from circa 1100 to 500 BC. They are part of a set of nesting coffins. Two coffins are displayed at the museum, while the third sits on view at Norton Simon Museum in Pasadena, California. The sarcophagi at the Museum of World Treasures are on long-term loan.

The outer coffin includes a dome-shaped lid with drawings painted in red, yellow, green, and white on its sides. Its cover is decorated with images of kneeling figures of Nut wearing a sun disk and holding ostrich plumes. According to ancient Egyptian mythology, Nut,

*The Egyptian goddess, Amun, is painted on a coffin housed at the Museum of World Treasures. Photo courtesy of Museum of World Treasures.*

pronounced "newt," is considered the goddess of the sky and heavens.

Also on display at the museum, the middle coffin includes the deceased's face painted on the lid. Inside is an image of a standing goddess with her arms outstretched. She is wearing a close-fitting red dress ornamented with a leaf motif pattern in blue and white.

Moreover, the mummy coffins are unique because they have an American Civil War connection. How could that be? They were purchased and brought to the United States in honor of John Griswold, who manufactured the steel plates used on the famous USS *Monitor* ironclad vessel built for the Union Navy.

---

**MUSEUM OF WORLD TREASURES**

**WHAT:** Exhibit

**WHERE:** 835 E 1st St.

**COST:** $9.95 for adults, $8.95 for seniors (65+), $7.95 for kids ages 4–12, free for kids ages 3 and under

**PRO TIP:** The *Ancient Egypt* exhibit is viewable during the museum's regular hours. Ask about Midnight at the Museum Camp-Ins that give kids an unforgettable experience sleeping among the coffins in the exhibit.

---

The museum only recently learned that the coffins were separated at one point, and the third, innermost, coffin was located at another museum in California.

# BIRD CHARACTERS

**What could be made with one million tiny tiles?**

It surely caught your eye if you've traveled on 17th Street near the south end of Wichita State University's campus. From far away, the massive mural resembles illustrated figures. But when seen up-close, its tiny tiles come into focus, revealing artist Joan Miró's remarkable handiwork.

How did the 80-pound mural, using one million tiny pieces of colorful Venetian glass, end up on the side of the school's Ulrich Museum of Art? University president Dr. Clark Ahlberg tasked Dr. Martin Bush with obtaining a significant work of art for the campus. Private donors paid for the project; before you knew it, the ball was rolling.

Miró, a renowned Spanish artist best known for combining abstract art with surrealism, was commissioned for the mural. He created *Personnages Oiseaux* (Bird People) using 80 panels measuring three by five feet each. Tile is heavy when used in mass. Each panel weighed 155 pounds. In 1978, the building's bricks were removed to make space for each panel. Thanks to the ingenuity

---

### PERSONNAGES OISEAUX

**WHAT:** Public art

**WHERE:** 1845 Fairmount St.

**COST:** Free

**PRO TIP:** Visitor parking at WSU is free on evenings and weekends. The Ulrich Museum offers dedicated free parking spaces just south of the museum's entrance on the east side of Fairmount, designated by red signage.

---

The project was more or less kept a secret until it was unveiled. Miró was an aging artist with health issues, so the university kept *Personnages Oiseaux* under wraps until it was complete.

*Artist John Miró initially designed* Personnages Oiseaux *as a small oil painting, and it eventually became a mural. Each of the tiles consists of hand-cut glass and marble.*

of construction professionals and engineers, it was successfully installed.

What do you make of the bird characters in their abstract forms? Try a different perspective if you're standing in front of the mural. Use the viewing station located south of WuShock Drive near the millipede sculpture to get a closer glimpse of Miró's tile work.

If visiting Monday through Saturday, art lovers should walk indoors at the Ulrich Museum of Art to view its latest exhibitions. Tours are self-guided at the museum and offer free admission. Groups should make a reservation for in-gallery or Outdoor Sculpture Collection tours led by a teaching docent.

# GNOME SWEET GNOME

**Where does one store over 100 gnomes when they don't have a garden?**

Hopping Gnome Brewing Company is quite possibly the only place in the city with the most extensive collection of garden gnomes. Throughout the taproom, the fat-bellied ceramic creatures sit on shelves, peek from behind glassware, and nestle into plant pots. More gnomes stare up at patrons from behind the bar's glass surface. The little guys can't be missed.

As the story goes, owners Torrey and Stacy Lattin were undecided about their new brewery's name. One night, Torrey was enjoying a beer at home when he noticed a giveaway during the 2012 Kansas City Royals All-Star Game, featuring a small gnome statue. Immediately, he was inspired to name the business Hopping Gnome since gnomes are known for drinking. It was decided. Since then, the gnome collection in the brewery's taproom has continued to grow.

What is it about the miniature men that makes them so appealing? Garden gnomes were first produced in Germany in the 1800s using clay. The mythology of the gnomes says that they lived underground and worked as guardians over the treasure. And one could argue that the craft beer produced at Hopping Gnome is like liquid gold and worthy of protection.

Regular customers at the brewery earn "Gnomie" status, and many customers belong to the Mug Club. Members of the club spend $100 to get a mug with 22-ounce pours for the price of 16-ounce pours all year long. Like the folklore creatures who love to partake, Gnomies

---

**HOPPING GNOME BREWING COMPANY**

**WHAT:** Brewery

**WHERE:** 1719 E Victor St.

**COST:** $6–7/beer

**PRO TIP:** The brewery's annual Festivus celebration is a popular event. Arrive early to score a seat at the bar.

*Is this gnome using a magnifying glass because he is looking for treasure or another beer?*

are devoted fans of the brewery's flagship beers and rotating taps. When the owners announced expanding the microbrewery to include a larger taproom, Gnomies showed up in droves to the anniversary party to cheer on the news.

---

Gnome statues appeared in Europe in the early 1600s and were considered a sign of good luck.

# KEEN ON HISTORY

**Is it a hotel or a museum?**

Hotel at Old Town occupies what was once the Keen Kutter building, home of one of Wichita's top-producing manufacturers of tools for Simmons Hardware Company in the early 1900s. Guests are transported back to 1906 through the hotel's double doors.

As a company, Keen Kutter was a pioneer in many ways. The four-story building was constructed to be strong and virtually waterproof. At the time, the warehouse was the largest in the world. It needed to be a massive building to produce the best quality tools on the market used by workers ranging from carpenters and farmers to gardeners and mechanics. The company's catalogs featuring the tools were the first to use color photography.

When the building was no longer used as a warehouse, local hotelier Jack DeBoer managed its restoration. In 1999, Hotel at Old Town welcomed guests for the first time. The museum-like hotel's interior celebrates the hardware company's significant contribution to the city's history. Glass display boxes on every floor near the elevators showcase vintage tools and cutlery. Framed black and white photos of Wichita's past decorate the hallway walls. The faces staring back from the pictures include entrepreneurs like Walter H. Beech and Lloyd Stearman, who helped make The Air Capital of the World what it is today. Appropriately, aviation books rest on tables in the lounge, waiting to be read by hotel guests.

---

The building's tower held 20,000 gallons of water to deliver to sprinklers in the event of a fire. A ghost sign of the Keen Kutter logo still is visible on the tower, which now serves as the hotel's elevator shaft.

*Hotel at Old Town, once the Keen Kutter building, is one of several surviving buildings in Wichita's Historic Warehouse District.*

## HOTEL AT OLD TOWN

**WHAT:** Building

**WHERE:** 830 E 1st St. N

**COST:** Free to tour

**PRO TIP:** Enjoy a classic cocktail from the hotel's bar, the 1906 Lounge. Raise a glass to the company's original founders pictured in a framed photo on a nearby wall.

Yet, the hotel also includes modern design touches. Oversized murals by local artist Steve Murillo depict the city's past in the hotel's lobby. A Keepers on Parade statue painted with images of Keen Kutter tools stands across from the reception desk.

# PEACEFUL PLAZA

**Where can one escape the hustle of downtown and be surrounded by waterfalls and ducks?**

In a tiny corner of downtown Wichita lies a delightful spot to watch nature amid artwork. The Kiva Plaza courtyard at the Garvey Center is a place some people may walk right through on their way to and from work without recognizing its beauty.

Tom Montemurro's sculpture *Sky-Earth-Medicine* is the anchor of the outdoor space, which includes a water pool at its base that ducks often visit. A graduate of Wichita State University, Montemurro is a Wisconsin-based sculptor who welds various metals with a torch. The 1974 sculpture depicts a life-size Native American on a horse, which community leader Olive W. Garvey commissioned. Standing 11 feet high and 8 feet long, it keeps with the Kiva theme, since "kiva" as an Indian term translates to "meeting place." And the plaza is not only a meeting place for people.

It's been the home of the Garvey Ducks for decades. The ducks know to return to it because it's where they can always count on finding birdseed strewn in large piles along the sidewalk by their caretaker, Laurie. The ducks

## GARVEY CENTER

**WHAT:** Courtyard

**WHERE:** 250 W Douglas Ave.

**COST:** Free

**PRO TIP:** Visit Kiva Plaza before 4 p.m. to glimpse the Garvey Ducks. Park via on-street parking or pay for parking in the Garvey Garage.

---

Tom Montemurro drove to Milwaukee to pick up the metal used to create his *Sky-Earth-Medicine* sculpture after he was not able to source bronze sheet in Wichita or Kansas City in the early 1970s.

*Garvey Center is home to a colorful mural, fountains, sculpture, and indoor art galleries making it an oasis in downtown Wichita.*

are released from a climate-controlled room at the center to the courtyard's fountain twice a day. They enjoy leisurely swims and meals until they are brought back to their room, around 4 p.m. The Garvey Ducks are fixtures of the fountain and small pond surrounding the statue.

# THE SKY'S THE LIMIT

**Are those vegetables growing on the roof of the parking garage?**

RISE Farms grows produce, herbs, and flowers five floors above downtown Wichita on the rooftop of a parking garage. In partnership with Fidelity Bank, horticulture expert Leah Dannar-Garcia from Firefly Farm and a team of employees tend to garden beds and greenhouse operations year-round. It is considered one of the largest rooftop farms in the Midwest.

Powered by a 204-panel solar setup, the 12,500-square-foot urban farm works to supply area restaurants. The operation is set up to be an urban extension of a mission of sustainable farming practices. Vegetables from cucumbers and eggplants to tomatoes and beets are grown in irrigated garden boxes. After the plants are started from seed inside the greenhouse, the seedlings are relocated outdoors to soak up sunlight and finish the growing cycle. Heaters inside a hoop house allow plants to grow despite frigid outdoor temperatures.

The produce grown at RISE Farms is used at First Mile Cantine, a restaurant at the bottom of the car park building. The nearby Grow plant shop uses the farm's botanicals and herbs in cocktail recipes.

The staff provides complimentary tours upon request. As you exit the parking garage elevator and walk out into RISE Farms, the aroma of fresh herbs and the sound of flying pollinators greet you.

---

The Kansas Department of Commerce recognized the rooftop farm with a To The Stars: Kansas Business Award as the South Central winner in the regional agribusiness category.

*Fidelity Bank's high-rise building can be seen in the backdrop of RISE Farms's wildflower garden. The flowers are used to attract pollinators like bees.*

Workers will pause from tending the gardens and harvesting vegetables to answer any questions. Who knows, you may walk away with fresh produce to take home.

## RISE FARMS

**WHAT:** Farm

**WHERE:** 320 S Market St.

**COST:** Free to tour from May 1– September 30

**PRO TIP:** You can purchase RISE Farms produce at locally owned GreenAcres.

# STANDING PROUDLY

**How many Keepers on Parade can you locate in the city?**

Like the *Keeper of the Plains* statue at the confluence of the Arkansas rivers, micro versions of the iconic figure are located all over the city. Keepers on Parade is a public art project that commissions the work of local artists to paint 10-foot-tall fiberglass replicas with approved designs. The project, which launched by Together Wichita to mark the city's 150th birthday, has flourished since its inception. Each artist is paid $1,000 to design and paint a statue.

### KEEPERS ON PARADE

**WHAT:** Public Art

**WHERE:** Citywide

**COST:** Free

**PRO TIP:** Ready to go on a driving tour of the Keepers on Parade? Use the online or printable map at togetherwichita.com to locate them. Tag #Keeper150 in your social media posts.

The colorful, towering structures stand proudly in parks, on location at museums, on schools' grounds and at local businesses. One never knows when you might spot one of the more than 60 statues installed in all parts of the city. Whether someone spontaneously locates one or uses the interactive online map during a self-guided tour, they'll soon notice how each Keeper's intricate colors and imagery match its surroundings. Some artists use

---

Keepers on Parade also can be found indoors in locations like Northeast Magnet High School or Hotel at Old Town, while others are placed outdoors, like the one at Advanced Learning Library designed for the city's mayor.

broad brushstrokes, while others apply their designs using spray paint. The iconic Wichita flag, sunflowers, or the city's recognizable skyline appear in designs. On occasion, the statues have fallen victim to vandals, requiring repair or replacement. A clear coating is added to each statue, making graffiti easier to remove.

*In Pursuit by Marilyn Williams stands on display at Exploration Place. The artist chose scenes of Native Americans, referencing the tribes that lived on the land near the Arkansas River.*

# WARBIRD WONDER

**Which military bomber contributed to the city's Air Capital of the World nickname?**

If one closes their eyes in the presence of Doc, a B-29 Superfortress, one might imagine the sounds of rivet guns and aircraft employees hurriedly working. In 1944, the production of World War II warbirds was at its height, and Doc and thousands of bombers were rolling off the production line at Boeing. The mission? To defeat Japan. It could fly higher and faster than any aircraft.

Doc rolled off the assembly line in March 1945 and was delivered to the United States Army. Within five months, it was used to drop two atomic bombs on Japan. It was part of a squadron of airplanes named after Snow White's Seven Dwarfs and the Wicked Witch, thus the name Doc.

At B-29 Doc Hangar, Education, & Visitors Center, the Superfortress rests in its permanent home when not taking to the skies to attend nationwide aviation shows. What makes Doc's

### B-29 DOC HANGAR, EDUCATION, & VISITORS CENTER

**WHAT:** Aircraft

**WHERE:** 1788 S Airport Rd.

**COST:** $10 per person +$5 for cockpit access, $20 per family up to five people +$10 for cockpit access

**PRO TIP:** Want to go for a ride in Doc? The B-29 Doc Flight Experience allows passengers to listen to a crew briefing, learn about its history, and take to the skies at 8,000 feet. Prices vary based on the seat position chosen, ranging from $600 to $1,500 each.

---

Boeing made 44 percent of all the B-29s produced by four factories, and Doc is one of 1,644 bombers manufactured in Wichita.

*The last of two remaining fly-worthy military bombers, Doc sits on display at B-29 Doc Hangar, Education, & Visitors Center. The other air-worthy Superfortress, FiFi, is based at the Victor N. Agather Hangar at Dallas Executive Airport.*

second life a wonder to aviation historians? The B-29 was restored after it rested in the Mojave Desert for over four decades and was used as target practice by the US Navy before an aviation enthusiast discovered it.

When aviation enthusiast Tony Mazzolini rescued it, the Navy said he couldn't buy it. Instead, they traded Doc for a B-25 that Mazzolini found in South America. He returned the damaged B-29 to its original home in Wichita using flatbed trailers. Volunteers were ready to work restoring Doc but had their work cut out for them. They spent over 16 years restoring the rare World War II bomber to pristine condition and airworthy status.

The warbird wonder makes an impression when seen up-close, especially in flight. When not stationed at B-29 Doc Hangar, Education, & Visitors Center, the aircraft frequently appears at air shows nationwide.

# A SEW-PHISTICATED PLACE

**What should a seamstress do with hundreds of unused sewing machines?**

The Sewing History Museum occupies the first floor of a historic home, a time capsule to an earlier era. Not only are the machines on display a testament to product engineering, but each also comes with a story. Some of the machines were donated, while others were acquired by founder Katrina Stockton. She was the city's first female tailor/seamstress who specialized in men's and women's alterations and custom designs, and she operated The Alteration Shoppe for 50 years.

Walking through the rooms of the last 1800s home, one learns that each machine tells the story of the Industrial Revolution, product design evolution, and brand innovation. Sewing machines date back to the oldest model, a 1909 Davis sewing machine from England that was once gifted to a woman as a wedding present. A dress near a machine shows the handiwork of another seamstress. A handkerchief demonstrates the talent and creativity of another.

Howe, Franklin, White, Singer, and Davis are some brands on

> **SEWING HISTORY MUSEUM**
>
> **WHAT:** Museum
>
> **WHERE:** 1230 N Waco Ave.
>
> **COST:** $15 for adults, $10 for seniors & students age 12 and up, $5 for kids age 6–11 years
>
> **PRO TIP:** Dedicate an hour for a guided tour of the museum or elect to peruse the museum at your own pace with an information pamphlet in hand.

The Chapman-Noble House was listed on the National Register of Historic Places in Sedgwick County on November 1, 2006.

display, ranging in age from 1900s hand-cranked machines to modern-day versions made of plastic with push-button controls. The museum's mission is to provide an environment for education and exploration of the history of sewing while inspiring an interest in the craft's artistry.

Why are curved presser feet used on children's sewing machines? Why was Singer an innovator in the industry? What prompted Coleman, a Wichita-founded outdoor company, to design a Coleman Model 4A Instant Lite Gas Iron? Stockton is eager to share facts like these with museum visitors.

The Queen Anne–style historic home, the museum's site, was designed and built in 1888 by William Henry Sternberg. He came from New York to Wichita in 1877 because of the booming economy. He also designed and built the Sedgwick County Courthouse and Campbell House (Castle Inn Riverside).

*The Sewing History Museum opened in March 2021 on N Waco Ave., a street that makes up the largest group of William Henry Sternberg designed-built homes in the United States.*

# SMALL SCREEN

**Could it be the city's smallest museum?**

When PBS Kansas moved to a more spacious location on the city's east side, it provided room to expand the public television station and add learning spaces, including what could be considered the city's smallest museum. What it lacks in size, Bonavia Foundation PBS Kansas Museum makes up for in significance.

   Not all broadcast studios have a room dedicated to displaying vintage equipment and memorabilia documenting its history. At PBS Kansas, public television fans can peer into glass cases containing the station's promotional merchandise and framed photos. A timeline wall decal wraps around the room, indicating important dates in the station's 50-year-plus history. Retired television cameras stand in a row as if ready to be put to use.

   The station, known for its local shows ranging from news broadcasts to documentaries, relies entirely on donations to stay in operation. One artifact worth noting in the museum is Irene Box's tin cup. An advocate of public television, she walked door to door collecting donations in the cup to contribute to the station's fundraising efforts in the 1970s. For lovers of PBS programs or broadcast journalism teachers, the museum offers an appreciative glimpse into the station's journey from its beginnings to the present day.

   Like its museum, the new facility was designed to bring the public into the station for other purposes. Adjacent to the broadcast museum, the Cochener-Garvey Children's Education & Discovery

---

Past employees, PBS Kansas viewers, and community members donated some of the items in the station's museum.

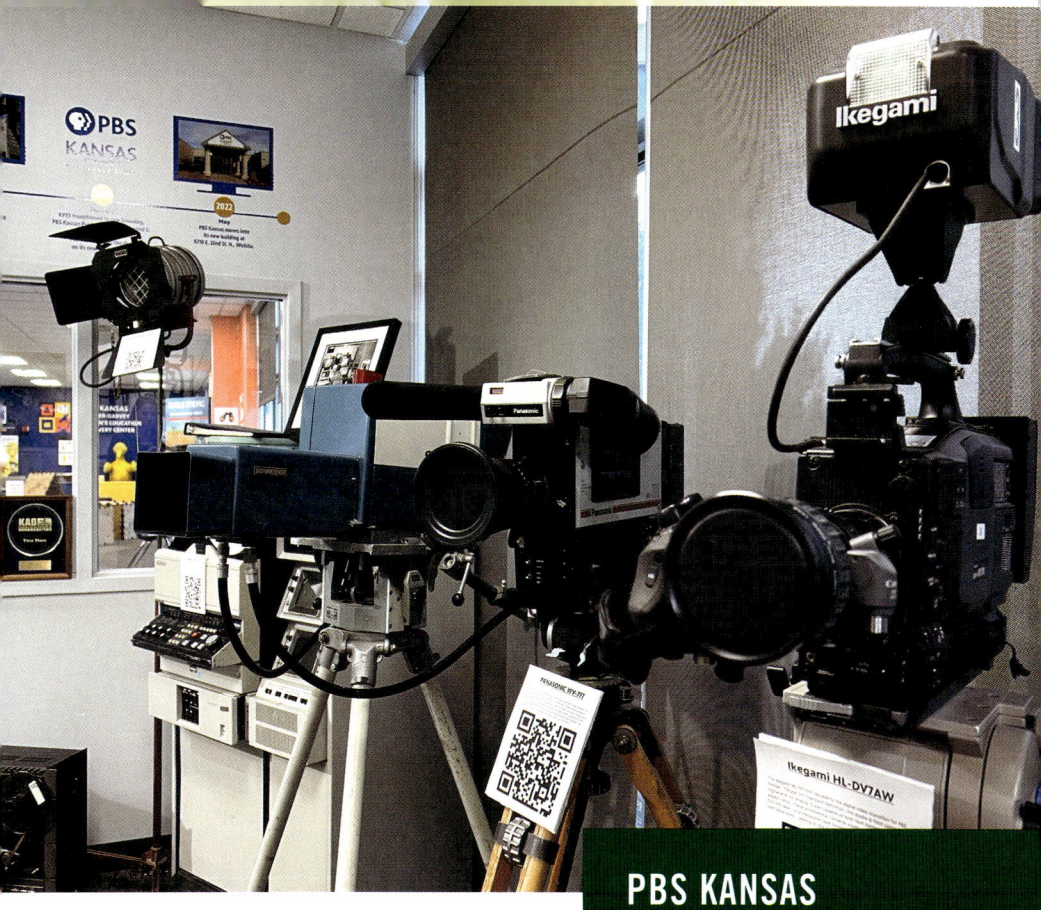

*A vintage Ikegami HL-DV7AW camcorder, along with other professional broadcast cameras, was used by PBS Kansas to record Channel 8 programming.*

Center is open during the week. Kids ages 2 through 10 are encouraged to use the hands-on displays to foster their creativity through art and reading. A small green room becomes a television area for kids to learn broadcasting.

## PBS KANSAS

**WHAT:** Museum

**WHERE:** 8710 E 32nd St. N

**COST:** Free; donations accepted. Sign in at the reception desk.

**PRO TIP:** Use your phone's camera to scan the QR codes attached to the museum's artifacts to learn more about each.

# BACK ALLEY ARTWORK

**What do flowers in bloom, a man in glasses, and a crane have in common?**

 A typical downtown alley in a city isn't always the most sought-after walkway. But Wichita's alleyways may surprise you. Some back-of-building doors at more than a dozen businesses feature colorful scenes created by artists.

Downtown Wichita launched the Alley Doors Project art initiative in 2020 to increase foot traffic and improve the downtown area's aesthetic. The project was inspired by a similar street art initiative launched in Louisville, Kentucky. Using a grant from the Knight Foundation Fund via the Wichita Community Foundation, doors located in the downtown corridor became urban art destinations. How were the designs chosen? Each participating business owner chose their favorite artist submission.

The discovery-driven urban gallery features distinctive designs ranging from nature images to abstract art. A crane spreads its wings in *Quivera Sunset* by Marcia K. Scurfield on Wasabi Hinkaku's back door. *Jazzy Man* by John Pirtle adjusts his glasses on the east side of Jury Eye Care's building. These designs and many others are displayed year-round and serve as must-see destinations during a self-guided tour during First Friday. Art lovers will notice a red information sign with the artist's name and the work's title located near each alley door.

---

Only Kansas-based artists can contribute to the online artwork database to be considered for the Alley Doors Project.

*One of many masterpieces located downtown, John Pirtle's Jazzy Man sports eyeglasses, which is appropriate since the door is at Jury Eye Care, 926 E Douglas Ave.*

## ALLEY DOORS PROJECT

**WHAT:** Public art

**WHERE:** Downtown Wichita

**COST:** Free

**PRO TIP:** Access the Alley Doors interactive map via downtownwichita.org to easily locate over a dozen door designs.

# FIREHOUSE FOOD

### When is it okay to light a fire at a fire station?

Station 8 BBQ looks like a typical two-story firehouse built in the 1920s: brick façade, arched doorways, garage doors with glass windows. It is a historic relic where brave firefighters listened for the alarm to jump into action, fight fires in the community, and save lives.

Today, something different is happening inside the building. Owner and chef Alex Eftekhar opened a restaurant in the space serving slow-smoked BBQ, and people are lining up at the door every day. A collector of vintage artifacts, Eftekhar filled the old firehouse with items purchased at auctions and donated by families of firefighters. On each booth sits a brass fire extinguisher.

Looking closely, one will also notice antiques of Wichita's past. The light poles came from Piccadilly Restaurant, a rare Kansas High Wheel Society bike is on hand, and dozens of lanterns made by Wichita-based The Coleman Company decorate the dining room. More seating is available on the outdoor patio, where an oversized buffalo, printing press, and tractor are in sight. Because why not? Across the street, three retired fire engines line up, including Engine 2, used by the Wichita Fire Department.

---

**STATION 8 BBQ**

**WHAT:** Restaurant
**WHERE:** 1100 E 3rd St. N
**COST:** $12–$26
**PRO TIP:** Arrive by 10:45 a.m. to be the first in line for ribs, which run out within an hour after the restaurant opens.

---

The Wichita Fire Department was the first all-motorized fire department in the United States and the second in the world.

*Built in 1928, Station 8 BBQ serves fresh-made meals inside a historic firehouse.*

Diners dig into trays stacked with succulent BBQ meats and scratch-made sides. Eftekhar and his team keep the fires ablaze in an outdoor smoker filled with traditional barbecue meat cuts.

While the smokers kick into overdrive, the kitchen crew busily prepares homemade pasta dishes and corn casserole—two of the most popular side dishes. Crave-worthy menu items include The Yeti, a sample of all the meats, and wagyu burnt ends.

# ANTIQUE ARTILLERY

**Why is a rare military cannon displayed in Central Riverside Park?**

Sometimes cities are gifted sculptures that are interesting but come with a story. The military cannon on display at Central Riverside Park was captured in the Spanish-American War in 1898 as a trophy and presented by the United States to Kansas, which then bestowed it to Wichita by Governor W. E. Stanley on June 15, 1900. The city's mayor, Finlay Ross, accepted the gift on behalf of the citizens on August 6, 1900. On the day the cannon was mounted on its stone base at the park, the local newspaper reported, "When the gun is properly mounted, it will be one of the most interesting adornments for the park that part of Wichita has."

Over the years, the cannon began to show signs of old age and use during the war. Eventually, it was restored, maintaining a hand-carved design into its muzzle and green patina finish. The rare cannon was reinstalled at the park's memorial in 2007.

Also a part of the memorial honoring the war, the cannon stands within walking distance of *The*

*The Spanish-American War memorial has been a fixture of Central Riverside Park since its installation, dating back to the 1900s.*

*Hiker*, a bronze statue made by Allen George Newman III in 1926. Dressed in a soldier's uniform and holding a rifle, the male figure represents a soldier in the Spanish-American War. Much fanfare preceded the statue's unveiling, including a Memorial Day parade with members of active military troops and veteran soldiers. Band musicians played during the singing of "America." During the ceremony, Kenneth W. Mathews delivered Lincoln's Gettysburg Address to people in attendance at the park.

## CENTRAL RIVERSIDE PARK

**WHAT:** Memorial

**WHERE:** 720 Nims St., near Murdock Street. Use on-street parking or a nearby available parking lot and walk to the memorial.

**COST:** Free

**PRO TIP:** Fascinated by war history? Drive a short distance to Veterans' Memorial Park at 339 Veterans Pkwy., which features seven memorials honoring United States veterans and Gold Star Mothers.

---

Frederick Funston, a military colonel who grew up in Iola, Kansas, ended the Philippine insurrection that followed the war with the help of the volunteer 20th Kansas Infantry Regiment.

# CREATIVE COMPLEX

**What would you draw with a pencil the size of a tree?**

The front entrance of The Art Park in east Wichita isn't hard to miss. Brightly colored pencils, pens, crayons, and paintbrushes seemingly emerge from the ground in front of the facility's parking lot. Passersby may do a double-take, but they soon realize that the tree trunks are carved to resemble a row of towering art supplies. From the grounds of The Art Park to the interior of its buildings, the complex is meant to inspire creativity.

Beyond the doors of The Art Park's white buildings on-site, teachers cultivate creativity with a host of classes and workshops for all ages, from preschoolers to older kids. From Young Chefs Cooking Class to Learning With Legos, parents and grandparents can select from a wide range of programs to enroll a child. Youngsters who love music will take lessons in a studio setting.

Kids Day Out is a popular summer event that receives rave reviews. Children can rotate between art and craft stations, play outside, and participate in physical education class or Kelcy's Dance Studio. Half-day and full-day registrations are available.

Outside, the campus playground is like a hidden treasure between two buildings. An oversized jungle gym and bright red choo-choo train encourage play. Whimsical yard art and statuary outline a walking path.

---

The Art Park was voted a 2022 silver medalist in the summer camps category of the website Best of Wichita's annual publication.

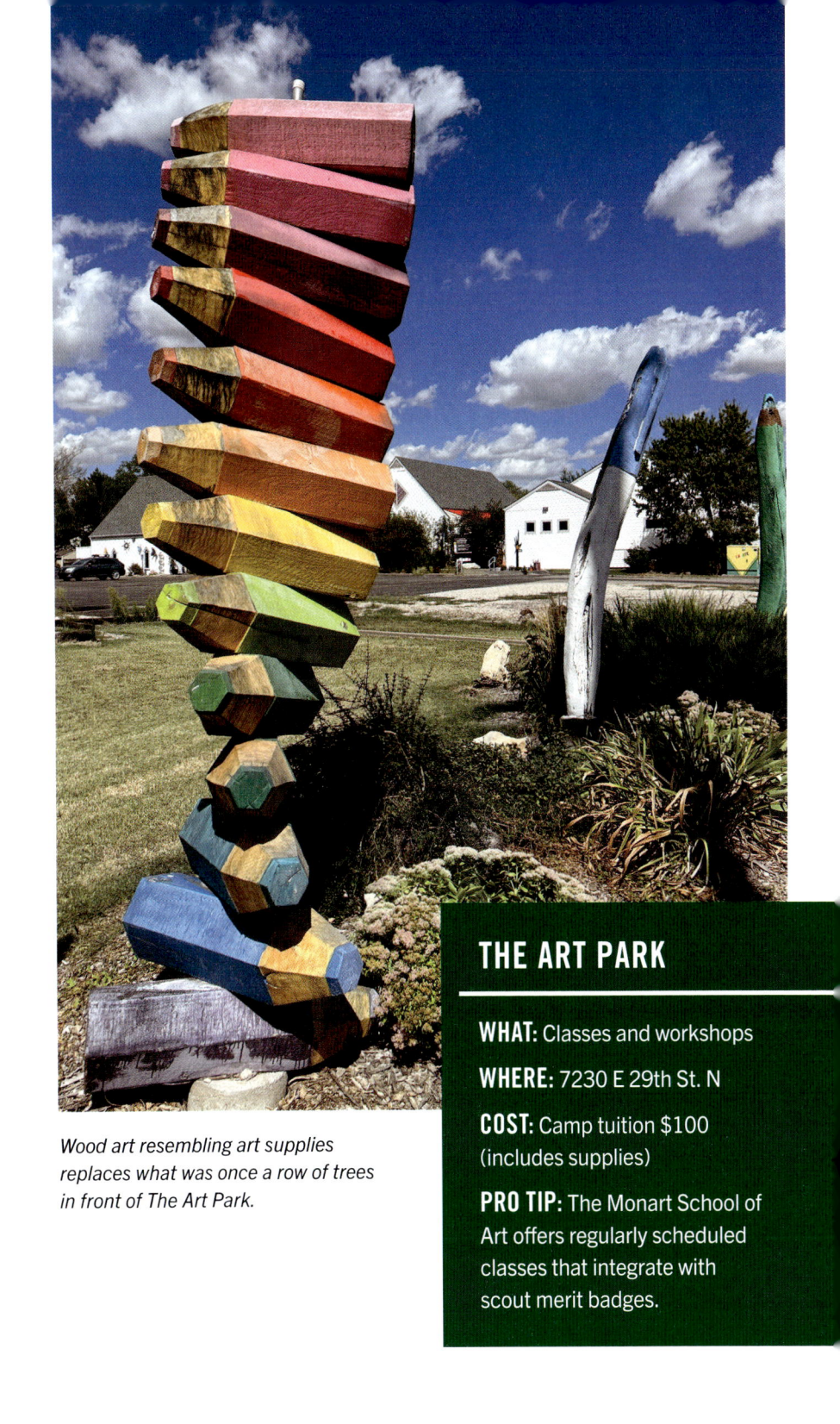

*Wood art resembling art supplies replaces what was once a row of trees in front of The Art Park.*

## THE ART PARK

**WHAT:** Classes and workshops

**WHERE:** 7230 E 29th St. N

**COST:** Camp tuition $100 (includes supplies)

**PRO TIP:** The Monart School of Art offers regularly scheduled classes that integrate with scout merit badges.

# WORK OF ART

**What kind of prairie grass doesn't move in the wind?**

What looks to be vertical metal pillars ascending from the ground in the Commerce Street Art District is an art installation, *Railgrass*. Made from old railroad tracks previously used in the area, it includes hundreds of yellow LED lights illuminating at night, resembling prairie grass. Better yet, a motion sensor near the railroad tracks detects when trains are passing by, causing *Railgrass* to flicker.

A project by the city to make over the space to include parking spaces and artwork, *Railgrass* was completed by artists Kent Williams and Stephen Atwood. Williams, a Wichita native who is "inspired by the genius of native plants and the metaphysics of freshwater ecosystems," is also cofounder of the artist cooperative Fisch Haus. Atwood, a collaborator on the project, is a Wichita State University sculpture major and owner of Atwood Studio.

The site of the artwork was once a space that abounded with discarded trash and piles of dirt. Williams spearheaded the revitalization project to beautify the area and add much-needed parking stalls. Now, the backlot space is less of an eyesore and more awe-inspiring because of the *Railgrass* artwork and thoughtful urban planning. A lone burr oak tree shades a nearby concrete concert stage. Below the tree, the urban oasis design includes lines of poetry inscribed into a metal grate below. The

---

The purpose of the art installation was to incorporate light as a primary design element to reinvigorate the area, known for its commercial businesses that include art galleries and antique stores.

Railgrass, *an art installation in the Commerce Art District and across from INTRUST Bank Arena, lights up in a yellow hue at night.*

## RAILGRASS

**WHAT:** Art Installation

**WHERE:** 400 S Commerce St.

**COST:** Free

**PRO TIP:** If attending an event at INTRUST Bank Arena, walk south across Waterman St. to the art installation to see it illuminated after the sun goes down.

inscription by poet Carter Revard reads, "It will not end, we sang in time, or leads of paper will be dancing lightly. Making a nation of the sun and other stars." Keeping with the railroad theme, a logo on the front of the performance stage pays tribute to the Atchison, Topeka, and Santa Fe Railway.

# COLORFUL CRAFTSMANSHIP

**What is that building up ahead?**

Bits of glass reflect the Kansas sun. Blue tile contrasts with gold adornments. An archway formed by dragon heads serves as an entrance.

A place of worship for Buddhists, the temple on Greenwich Road is an eye-catching structure that many people don't realize is there unless they travel south of Kellogg. The Lao Buddhist Associates of Kansas complex features multiple buildings on its grounds, but the towering temple makes road trippers want to pull over. Painted in metallic gold, reds, and yellows, the worship center is the focal point of the five-acre property. The monks living on the property added decorative elements on the outside of the building, casting them in concrete and then applying them to the structure.

According to National Geographic, Buddhists "believe that the human life is one of suffering, and that meditation, spiritual and physical labor, and good behavior [are] the ways to

---

## LAO BUDDHIST ASSOCIATES OF KANSAS

**WHAT:** Architecture

**WHERE:** 2550 S Greenwich Rd.

**COST:** Free

**PRO TIP:** Visit the Lao Buddhist Associates of Kansas's Facebook page to learn more about upcoming events that are open to the public with free admission. The complex welcomes anyone who wants to focus on inner peace.

---

Buddhist temples include an image or statue of the Buddha, and temple design focuses on five elements: Earth, Wisdom, Fire, Air, and Water.

*Elaborately decorated, handpainted dragons flank the entrance to the temple at Lao Buddhist Associates of Kansas.*

achieve enlightenment, or nirvana." The monks at Lao Buddhist Associates of Kansas spent endless hours beautifying the meditation center and temple, an undeniable example of ornate architecture. They openly invite visitors to admire the temple and, if so moved, to join them in meditation or ask questions.

Construction is ongoing at the Lao Buddhist Associates of Kansas complex to eventually accommodate visiting monks.

# FROM THE ASHES

**Why are three columns standing proudly on the hill?**

Students of Wichita State University (WSU), once named Fairmount College, may have walked past three lone columns on campus innumerable times without realizing why the remnants of an old building are a focal point of the university's landscape. The Carnegie Columns are what remains of Fairmount College's Carnegie Library, destroyed by fire in 1964.

The Carnegie Library was designed by Albert R. Ross and Nathan J. Morrison, Fairmount College's first president, who made it a goal to build a library for the college. Morrison died in 1907.

The portico and eight columns remained in place until 1973, when the ruins was cleared to build McKnight Arts Center. Three columns and lintels with the cornerstone were moved on April 28, 1973, to the location where they stand today. A time capsule also was buried there. Its contents were revealed when it was opened during the university's centennial in 1995. What was inside? The capsule contained materials interred at the library's cornerstone-laying on March 10, 1908. At its base, an inscription added on May 3, 1996, reads, "Standing Proudly On The Hill."

A 1936 graduate, Kathleen Edmonton, played a role in raising money to preserve the columns in 1972. Her daughter Kelly Callen said in an interview with local reporter Carla Eckels that at one point, her mother stood in front of the columns, refusing to

---

A phrase from the school's alma mater reads,
 Our Alma Mater Wichita,
 Stands Proudly on the hill.
 Our sons and daughters bow to thee,
 Our hearts will praise we fill.

*The site where the columns stand today on the Wichita State University campus was considered the highest point of land in Sedgwick County.*

let the bulldozers take them down. "The Carnegie was her passion. We're very fortunate to still have these. They're very regal. At one time this was the entrance to the WSU at 17th and Fairmount. It was a nice entrance to the university, and they're just nice to have. They're kind of fun. She really was amazing."

## WICHITA STATE UNIVERSITY

**WHAT:** Carnegie Columns

**WHERE:** 17th and Fairmount St.

**COST:** Free

**PRO TIP:** Locate the Morrison Library Marker dedicated to Nathan Morrison, founder and president of Fairmount College from 1895–1907, located on Alumni Dr. when traveling north. The marker is at the main entrance of Morrison Hall, about 200 feet southeast of the intersection of Alumni Dr. and Perimeter Rd.

# OPEN-FACED FUN

**Should diners be concerned about a rhino in a restaurant?**

Wichita has plenty of restaurants for diners to choose from, but City Bites, in particular, delivers an element of unpredictability for visitors who choose to dine in. Unlike fast-casual restaurants that can resemble each other, the interior of this Wichita destination delivers a good-humored design. As one Google reviewer noted, "the interior decor is like a cross between *Beetlejuice* and *Jumanji*."

For decades, diners have enjoyed sandwiches and freshly baked cookies surrounded by quirky wall art. A replica of a rhino appears to burst through a wall. A five-ton cannonball moves back and forth from the ceiling as if to caution diners of its impending fall. The dining room's walls are decorated with brightly colored geometric patterns, adding to the restaurant's overall whimsical style. But it's the bathroom's witty design that trumps the rest. One step inside the restroom, and diners are in for an entertaining surprise. Consider this a warning.

The menu portions, like the restaurant's interior design, will exceed your expectations. The stuffed baked potatoes are so large they look to be the size of

---

## CITY BITES

**WHAT:** Restaurant

**WHERE:** 3570 N Woodlawn St., Ste. 500

**COST:** $7–$14

**PRO TIP:** Skip the drive-through for an unforgettable indoor dining experience.

---

City Bites is an Oklahoma-based restaurant chain with nearly 20 locations. The company started as an 800-square-foot restaurant run by three brothers in 1986.

*Expect the unexpected inside the City Bites restaurant on the city's east side.*

footballs. Heaping deli sandwiches are loaded to the max with sliced meat, cheese, and vegetables. The bread is baked fresh daily from the kitchen's oven. Still hungry? The staff makes scratch-made soft cookies the size of small dinner plates.

# PERFECTED PIZZA

**What recipes are responsible for earning a family billions of dollars?**

Sometimes the best recipes are kept under lock and key and remain secret for only the family to use. Such is not the case with Dan and Frank Carney, brothers who founded Pizza Hut in Wichita. The restaurant's original pizza sauce recipe was written on a paper napkin, and its replica is displayed in the Pizza Hut Museum on the Wichita State University campus.

What did two college guys know about making pizza in June 1958? Not much, it turns out. With $600 donated by their mom, they invested in the business. The Carney brothers learned how to make the sauce and dough from their sister's friend, John Bender. The sauce was a no-brainer. Spices and tomatoes were added to a base made with onions, green peppers, celery, and garlic to create the sauce. And how about the crust? Bender had never made the dough before. After making French bread dough from the recipe book *Encyclopedia of Cooking*, Bender rolled out the dough thin and the pizza crust baked to a crisp. If museumgoers look inside the glass case located to the right of the recipe case, it contains the rolling pin the Carney brothers used in the first Pizza Hut to flatten and shape the dough.

---

The night the guys prepared the pizza dough for the first time, they mixed it in a baby's bathtub.

*The mother of Pizza Hut's founders, Beverly Carney, suggested the name "Pizza Hut" when the building's small sign could only hold eight letters.*

## PIZZA HUT MUSEUM

**WHAT:** Museum

**WHERE:** 2090 Innovation Blvd.

**COST:** Free

**PRO TIP:** Museum visitors may park north of the building in the Marcus Welcome Center parking lot, or west of it by Eck Stadium.

Pizza Hut grew from a $600 start-up business to one of the world's biggest, most well-known restaurant companies. The company's net worth totaled over $810 billion at the time of this book's publication. During the early days of Pizza Hut, Bender was offered a one-time partnership in the business in exchange for his recipe and for teaching the Carneys to make pizza.

133

# GAS LAMP GRIDIRON

**Whose bright idea was it to play a football game at night?**

Imagine watching a football game at night illuminated only by gaslit lamps. College football fans did just that in 1905 during a Cooper (now Sterling College) vs. Fairmount (now Wichita State University) game at Association Field. It was a historical night. Not only was it the first night football game played west of the Mississippi, but Fairmount also triumphed over Cooper 24-0. The original site of Association Park is at Levy Street (now Mount Vernon) and Main Street.

Considered an "experiment," The Coleman Company furnished portable, gas-powered lanterns to light up the field. A sports editorial in the *Wichita Beacon* on October 7, 1905, reported the game was well-attended; however, watching the action on the field was brutal. "There were hundreds on the sidelines who, without any hesitancy, stated that they had not even seen the ball [at] all during the game." According to the columnist, "This was not football; it may be termed anything else, but certainly can never

### COOPER VS. FAIRMONT FOOTBALL GAME

**WHAT:** Land

**WHERE:** Mount Vernon and Main Sts.

**COST:** Free

**PRO TIP:** Wichita State University does not have a football team; however, fans of the game can root for Wichita Force, a professional indoor football team.

---

Coleman purchased the patent for the Efficient Lamp from Irby-Gilliland Company and moved the Hydro-Carbon Light Company's headquarters to Wichita, Kansas, in 1902. The company's lamps illuminated the 1905 football game.

*Two Coleman lanterns made during the 1910s–1920s are part of a larger collection on display at Station 8 BBQ. Photo courtesy of Station 8 BBQ.*

take the place of the mighty daylight struggles, such as many of us have seen elsewhere."

Cooper struggled to compete with Fairmount's Wheatshockers, who made gains on nearly every play. They were not the only ones who struggled on the field that night. Reportedly, "the officials were hampered in their work on account of not being able to see the plays."

# RAINBOW RESIDENCES

**Where is one of the city's most popular photo backdrops?**

Kansas may be known as a place where one can follow the Yellow Brick Road, but in Wichita, locals know that one street, Rainbow Row, is the draw. Oakland Avenue, a residential street between Hillside and Rutan streets, is one-of-a-kind. The steep and curvaceous route resembles a street you might see in San Francisco, California.

The homes are distinctive within the College Hill neighborhood, mainly consisting of historic homes that maintain a classic, original design. But the most apparent difference? The color choices. The popular suburban area is lined with multiunit apartment complexes and two-story private homes painted in vibrant colors, unlike any other neighborhood in the city. Oakland Avenue's residences are more like stucco, differentiating them from more traditional houses in the area.

Located less than a three-minute drive to College Hill Park, this charming section of town offers affordable living in one of the city's trendy neighborhoods.

---

### RAINBOW ROW

**WHAT:** Houses

**WHERE:** Oakland Ave. between Hillside and Rutan Sts.

**COST:** Free

**PRO TIP:** Park on the north side of the street if visiting to stop and take a photo.

---

Like a street scene from a San Francisco neighborhood, the residential street often referred by Wichitans as Rainbow Row is a common place for photoshoots.

*Looking east on Oakland Ave., one notices a row of multistory apartment buildings painted in untraditional colors that appears distinctly different from other streets in the neighborhood.*

Other nearby places to visit include Crown Uptown, Clifton Square, and restaurants on Douglas Avenue.

Art lovers who appreciate Rainbow Row will also enjoy a self-guided tour of dozens of murals painted for the Douglas Design District project, accessible within walking distance of Oakland Avenue. Also, Keepers on Parade, miniature artistic replicas of the original *Keeper of the Plains*, are located throughout College Hill, adding to the creative vibe of the neighborhood.

# IPA IN AN IGLOO

**Where can you find a polar paradise in the city?**

Wichita may not look like the North Pole, but the igloos at Nortons Brewing Company are reminiscent of traditional polar housing during cold weather months. Visitors to the brewery can transport themselves to a winter wonderland by reserving a garden igloo adorned with holiday lights for the ultimate dining experience. Each one comfortably seats six people, and the temperature never dips to frigid temperatures, thanks to a small space heater resembling a mini fireplace.

Available for 1.5-hour or 3-hour blocks, the igloos are a cozy place to share conversation with family and friends while sipping a cocktail or craft beer. Servers unzip the igloo's entrance to deliver pretzel bites with beer queso, heaping sandwiches and fries, or appetizers like Bacon Crack. Guests can order from the entire dinner and drink menus. Keep the fun going by playing a board game. Uno™, anyone?

Nortons Brewing Company is known for doing things a bit differently. From their ever-changing beer taps selection to the eclectic atmosphere, diners

---

**NORTONS BREWING COMPANY**

**WHAT:** Garden igloos

**WHERE:** 125 St. Francis St.

**COST:** Check the brewery's website for current igloo rental pricing.

**PRO TIP:** The igloo's bluetooth speaker connects to a user's phone, allowing them to play the music of their choice.

---

The beer garden at Nortons Brewing Company transforms into a polar paradise during the winter season.

*Igloos are reserved for people ages 21 and older. No pets or smoking are allowed.*

can expect a unique experience at each visit. When the igloos are not on the outdoor patio, dog parents are encouraged to bring their four-legged friends and kids to join them. Yard games, a massive swing set, and live music on the outdoor stage keep it lively. Indoors, it's easy to play a game of I Spy. Skeletons, metal art, and one-of-a-kind art make it fun to dine on "scratch-made grub, served with love." Whether you're sipping an IPA with a Bacon Crack appetizer or enjoying a Train Wreck sandwich inside an igloo or the restaurant, the experience is unforgettable.

# HISTORIC HIDEAWAY

**What scenic spot is tucked away in one of the busiest downtown areas?**

If you walk too quickly down William Street, you may not realize it's there. Heritage Square Park is not a secret, but it could be considered a hidden gem in the central business district. Located in the shadow of historic City Hall (now Wichita-Sedgwick County Historical Museum) and Carnegie Library (now Fidelity Bank), it is a companion space to the museum, funded by the Junior League of Wichita.

Dedicated during America's bicentennial in 1976, its design was intentionally turn-of-the-century, featuring a sunken garden, water features, and vintage-looking light poles. Surrounded by ornamental fencing and an ornate gazebo, the courtyard and park feature thoughtfully chosen sculptures.

Sometimes casually referred to as "Naked Lady Park" by locals, the park's focal point is a bronze sculpture created by Salina artist Richard Bergen, *Heritage Woman*, emerging from a water feature. Another statue in the square, *Boy and the Boot*, arrived at the space with a storied past. It was initially purchased by Mayor Finlay Ross in 1898 as a gift to the city's children. Once considered a landmark in front of Riverside Park's pavilion, it was restored in 1921 after a vandal damaged it. Now, it takes up permanent residence just beyond the square's main entrance.

---

## HERITAGE SQUARE PARK

**WHAT:** Park

**WHERE:** 115 E William St.

**COST:** Free access on Sundays via the museum with no-cost admission. Otherwise, museumgoers pay admission to the building: $5 for adults, $2 for children ages 6–12, free for ages 6 and under

**PRO TIP:** Follow Wichita-Sedgwick County Historical Museum's Facebook event page for Heritage Square Concert Series announcements.

*The entrance to Heritage Square Park via the Wichita-Sedgwick County Historical Museum frames the courtyard's natural elements and one of its notable sculptures.*

Heritage Square Park's scenery flourishes in the spring when the landscape greens up and flowers bloom. It transforms into an ideal backdrop for events. The gazebo becomes a bandstand for local musicians to entertain audiences. Starting in September each year, the museum hosts the Heritage Square Concert Series on Wednesdays at noon. Admission is free over the lunch hour, and attendees are encouraged to bring a lunch.

---

The site of Heritage Square Park originally was the location of one of the city's early jails.

# MONUMENT MASTERPIECE

**Where can you honor service members who fought and died in the American Civil War?**

The Soldiers & Sailors Monument at the Old Sedgwick County Courthouse was built from 1912 to 1913 to honor the servicemen who fought and died in the Civil War. Designed by E. M. Viquesney, it was constructed to be a memorial to veterans. Each of the four statues was created by Frederick Cleveland Hibbard (1881–1950) and then mounted on the granite and marble pavilion. An American sculptor, Hibbard was well-known for designing Civil War memorials. The towering downtown monument is considered one of Kansas's premier Civil War monuments, and it was listed on the National Register of Historic Places in 1998.

The figures on the monument represent the Infantry, Calvary, Artillery, and Navy of the Union States, each weighing 800 to 1,100 pounds. At its highest point, a copper statue, *Liberty*, is dressed

### SOLDIERS & SAILORS MONUMENT

**WHAT:** Memorial

**WHERE:** 510 N Main St.

**COST:** Free

**PRO TIP:** After touring the monument, drive a short distance to Veterans Memorial Park (339 Veterans Pkwy.) to pay tribute to 18 memorials representing six wars.

---

The Soldiers & Sailors Monument's land was donated to the county by Julia P. Munger, the widow of one of the city's founders, Darius S. Munger. The original Munger home is available to view at Old Cowtown Museum.

*Initially, the figure at the top of the monument faced north instead of south. Union veterans wanted* Liberty *repositioned, at a cost of $100. The entire structure cost over $20,000 to build.*

in a gown, holding an unfurled flag and a laurel wreath symbolizing peace.

What makes the memorial more impressive is that inside the base's interior, designated as Memorial Hall, is where the county once housed Union Civil War memorabilia. Damp conditions in 1915 required the removal of the artifacts. The bronze doors of the Soldiers & Sailors Monument are decorated with an eagle and emblem reminiscent of Greek Revival architecture. According to the Smithsonian Institution Research Information System, Memorial Hall's museum-like interior contains display cases and bronze pilasters. An electrified brass chandelier is used to illuminate the interior.

Colonel J. N. Harrison, commander of the Grand Army of the Republic for Kansas, said at the unveiling ceremony, "It is fitting that such monuments as these should be erected to the memory of the heroes of that great struggle. But the men who fought are greater than the monuments. They still live in the hearts of their countrymen."

The memorial was rededicated on November 11, 2001, a Veterans Day event featuring Civil War reenactors, scout troops, speakers, music, and a gun salute.

# TUCKED-AWAY PARK

**Where can people visit a park in a city within the city?**

A beautiful yet humble park in a city within a city has remained a draw for nature seekers over the years. The City of Eastborough, incorporated in 1937, is a residential community with a long history.

How was a city established within the city? The residents elected seven officers, including Frank L. Dunn, who was unanimously elected mayor on July 15, 1937. He was a former mayor of Wichita. Eventually, a board of county commissioners gave Eastborough third-class city status. According to the *Wichita Eagle* on June 16, 1937, "the city covers about 425 acres and represents a total investment of approximately two million dollars." The population was about 200 residents within 48 homes, combining Woodlawn Heights and Eastborough. Since the small city's founding, it has maintained a government system and police force.

Wichitans regularly drive through the city often to make their way to Towne East Square while adhering to the posted 20 miles-per-hour speed limit signs. In the event they stop at the town's tucked-away Eastborough

> **CITY OF EASTBOROUGH**
>
> **WHAT:** Park
>
> **WHERE:** 34 Willowbrook Rd.
>
> **COST:** Free
>
> **PRO TIP:** The park is closed to the public from midnight–6 a.m. Be sure to park in a designated lot. Although tempting, feeding wildlife is prohibited.

The west entrance to the City of Eastborough displays a replica of Santa in a sleigh pulled by reindeer during Christmastime.

*Bronze statuary of children at play are positioned along the paved walking paths through Eastborough Park.*

Park, they are in for a treat. Visitors can stroll the tree-covered walkways while admiring bronze statuary and observing wildlife. Kids will appreciate the park's modern playground equipment near the pond. Bringing a picnic lunch for the family to enjoy outdoors? The park's covered gazebo is the ideal setting.

In the spring and summer, the park often serves as a scenic backdrop for portrait photographers to use. A popular spot for photos, a small waterfall cascades over rocks in the south corner of the pond. But the fun doesn't end when the weather turns cold. During the winter, ice-skating on the pond is allowed at one's own risk when posted, from 8 a.m. to 11 p.m.

# STONE STRUCTURE

**Where do you go when you want to rock out to music inside a building made of rock?**

As the years have progressed, some old buildings in the city have taken on a new life. The Scottish Rite Temple, built in 1887 and 1888 for the Young Men's Christian Association (YMCA), was sold to the Masons in 1898. From the outside, you'd never suspect it's the same place where concertgoers gather to rock out to local and nationally renowned musicians at TempleLive. The venue also hosts weddings and special occasion events.

What makes the Scottish Rite Temple the best place for a venue? Its awe-inspiring architecture and historical significance as a city landmark are a big draw. During its construction, buildings were popping up at a hurried pace in the city. Designed by Wichita architects Proudfoot and Bird, the three-story structure cost approximately $60,000.

Its Romanesque exterior design using native limestone was distinctly different from its roofline of tall chimneys and spires. An awe-inspiring interior includes a grand stairway, hand-beveled glass, and a third-floor art glass dome. Crown molding, crystal chandeliers, and wood floors hearken back to an earlier time in interior design. Visitors to The Egyptian Room are greeted with a semicircular wall of stained glass windows illuminated on a sunny day. Complete with balcony seating, the auditorium lends itself naturally to a concert hall used by TempleLive.

---

The architects who designed the building moved to Wichita during the 1880s building boom. Their first commissioned project was the Administration Building at Garfield University, now Friends University.

*From afar, the Scottish Rite Temple's architecture makes a statement among buildings in the downtown area. Its intricate details showcase ornate design, as seen in its south entrance bay window made of stained glass.*

## SCOTTISH RITE TEMPLE

**WHAT:** Venue

**WHERE:** 332 E 1st St. N

**COST:** Ticket prices $18–$49

**PRO TIP:** If you're interested in reserving the building for a private event, you can schedule a tour by emailing events@templelive.com.

Fans watch performances from wooden seats surrounded by elegant stained glass windows. In its early days, the auditorium was said to compete with the world's first opera houses "that any Broadway producer would be happy to have at his disposal." While live events are the draw, bringing music fans into the building today, the architecture is the showstopper.

The building was placed on the National Register of Historic Places in 1972.

# ANIMAL ART

**Where is a giant turtle with a medallion on its back hiding in the city?**

Some call it environmental art, while others call it a sculpture garden. One thing is for sure. Sedgwick County Art Walk is whimsical in style, emphasizing, well, just that: nature. Located adjacent to Sedgwick County Park, the outdoor exhibit features artwork inspired by its surroundings. Its purpose is to recognize the need for nature conservation. The work of six artists sits on 20 acres, serving as an interactive space for curious parkgoers and families in a natural setting.

A winding sidewalk serves as the *Turtle Maze*, designed by Tobin Rupe. Park attendees follow the winding sidewalk to the maze's center to discover a stone turtle designed by artist Terry Corbett with a medallion on its back. The bonus? The medallion is inscribed with a riddle. A 30-foot-tall totem

## SEDGWICK COUNTY ART WALK

**WHAT:** Public art

**WHERE:** Use the 13th St. entrance on the south side to park and look for the Sedgwick County Art Walk's sign. Parking is free. Handicapped-accessible.

**COST:** Free

**PRO TIP:** Inspired by nature? Don't forget to bring a camera with you to the park. Nature trails provide plenty of opportunities to photograph wildlife.

---

The county donated the land for the park. Nearby Sedgwick County Park is one of the city's largest parks, featuring fishing lakes. Anglers can purchase bait and tackle at the on-site supplies store.

*The Sedgwick County Art Walk is designed in the shape of a turtle from an aerial view.*

entitled *Endangered Species* by Gino Salerno showcases North American animals. A 125-foot-long steel Fossil Fish emerges from the Earth while another installation, *Crane Dance*, represents the bird's return from extinction. It was made using limestone from the Flint Hills.

Sedgwick County Art Walk is a small part of a larger outdoor setting, Sedgwick County Park. It is common to see residents biking along its trails, dropping a line into a fishing lake (license required!), or enjoying a picnic at open shelters.

# CITY'S LARGEST CIGAR

**Should you worry if you see smoke at a gas station?**

Since 1996, Mort's Martini and Cigar Bar has occupied a humble brick building that once stood as a gas station in the 1920s. The W. A. Jones Building was renovated into a lounge bar that serves patrons over 160 handcrafted martinis and an extensive beer selection.

The historic building is a hangout for cigar enthusiasts, who are encouraged to kick back and enjoy a stogie on the covered patio. Bar employees provide tableside cigar service when requested. Outdoor TVs make it possible to watch the game during daytime hours. Live bands entertain patrons while they clink glasses and talk among themselves every night. On Mondays, the place fills up quickly after work, with people taking advantage of half-price martinis.

Indoors, the vibe is just as chill. People sit at high-top tables across from the bar and underneath what has to be the city's largest cigar. One of the building's HVAC pipes became the inspiration for a faux cigar extending across the ceiling. An east-wall mural depicts a man

### MORT'S MARTINI AND CIGAR BAR

**WHAT:** Bar

**WHERE:** 923 E 1st St. N

**COST:** Martini pricing $7.50–$11.50

**PRO TIP:** Consider yourself a cigar aficionado. Mort's sells a large selection of cigars, and Old Town Cigars is within walking distance of the bar.

---

The Dominican Republic was a hot spot for making cigars in the 1990s, the same decade that Mort's opened in Old Town.

*Mort's bar patrons are known to regularly light up cigars at the bulding that was once a gas station located at First and Washington streets.*

smoking a cigar, while the west wall's glowing red-orange neon replicates the end of the fiery stogie.

One glance at the interior walls of the bar, and bargoers feel like they are part of a great community of Mort's fans. Every inch of wall space is covered in framed black-and-white photos of gleeful guests staring back at the camera.

# VICTORIOUS VOYAGE

**Why is a massive sailboat permanently displayed in a landlocked state?**

It makes perfect sense to have sailboats near water in front of a boathouse. The sailing vessel, *The Jayhawk*, is unique because it was the ship used in qualifying for the 1992 America's Cup, and it's on display downtown. Resting on a platform behind its permanent home at the Wichita Boathouse, *The Jawhawk* intrigues riverwalk visitors.

One of four yachts built for the racing syndicate, it was the brainchild of Bill Koch. He commanded *America3*, which went on to win the America's Cup in 1992. The Wichita businessman's team won the race by 44 seconds over the Italian vessel *Il Moro di Venezia*. On race day, the vessel was challenged by equipment issues, winds, and choppy seas. Considered an underdog in the sailing race, *America3* won it 4–1. As reported by the National Sailing Hall of Fame, Bill Koch's pursuit of victory came down to the science of sailing, focusing on hydrodynamic and aerodynamic technology. He said, "The boat that is going to win is the one that makes the fewest mistakes. Making no mistakes is a function of teamwork, not star power, but team power."

After the yacht was retired from competition, it toured the United States in an effort to promote sailing before it arrived in Wichita. Koch donated the first version of his winning sailboat, *The Jayhawk*, to the city, hoping it would inspire others. At one time, there were talks of relocating the sailboat to another area

---

Bill Koch grew up in Kansas and started sailing on a lake in Indiana before leaving to study at Massachusetts Institute of Technology (MIT).

*The Jayhawk rests on a platform at its permanent home, located behind the Wichita Boathouse, viewable from the Lewis St. riverwalk area. Stairs lead to an observation deck allowing visitors to peer inside the sailboat.*

## THE JAYHAWK

**WHAT:** Sailboat

**WHERE:** 515 S Wichita St.

**COST:** Free

**PRO TIP:** Interested in taking to the Arkansas River in a vessel much smaller than a sailboat? Boats and Bikes (150 N McLean Blvd.) rents kayaks, paddle boards, and pedal boats.

on the riverbank, but the sailboat remains at the Wichita Boathouse. In 2014, it was restored. The display case in the Wichita Boathouse, an event venue space that doubles as the Kansas Sports Hall of Fame, houses a miniature replica of the winning sailboat and photographs of its captain.

# BEYOND THE BOOKS

**How do you access a bar within a bar through a secret entrance?**

Sometimes the best secrets are kept behind closed doors. At The Brass Taproom, patrons must enter a speakeasy-style bar via a bookcase in the wall. Inspired by the style of establishments in the 1880s, the gathering space attracts bargoers in search of a laid-back bar experience.

Technically, The Brass Taproom is a bar within a bar. To access it, one must walk into Sidepockets, a billiards hall, and find the "door" that leads into the hidden lounge space. In one motion, the bookcase pulls open, revealing a Prohibition-style bar behind it. Like drinking establishments of the past, the interior resembles an old-style saloon with dark wood finishes and upscale pool tables. The Brass Taproom's low-lit vibes transport visitors back in time, from its tin ceiling to its backlit, faux windows. Historic photographs set the scene.

The bar is open to the general public on select evenings of the week when it's not reserved for a private event. Not only can one count on a long list of

### THE BRASS TAPROOM

**WHAT:** Bar

**WHERE:** 614 S Tyler Rd.

**COST:** Private meal catering $7.99–$9.99/person

**PRO TIP:** To reserve the event space for a private event, visit thebrasstaproom.com to access its calendar.

---

Drink specials served at Sidepockets are also available to patrons at The Brass Taproom. A fan of cocktails made with top-shelf liquor? Ask about the Reserve Collection.

*A neon sign above a nondescript bookcase serves as a clue, indicating the bar's entrance.*

available cocktails, but sports bar–themed food also is available from Sidepockets's menu. On occasion, live bands keep the bar atmosphere lively.

# PLAY BALL

**Where can you find hundreds of rare Wichita baseball artifacts in one place?**

Wichita baseball fans have a place to rejoice in the sport's history, the Wichita Baseball Museum. In fact, they may think they've died and gone to baseball heaven when they see items from the city's baseball past displayed from floor to ceiling. Located at Riverfront Stadium, home of the Wichita Wind Surge, the modern museum is where lovers of the game can admire rare Wichita baseball artifacts in one place. One can expect exhibits featuring items from Wichita's all-Black team, the Monrovians, the National Baseball Congress (NBC), and remnants of Lawrence-Dumont Stadium. On display is an original turnstile that thousands of fans passed through as they made their way into the stadium.

Lawrence Stadium opened in August 1934 with a formal dedication ceremony on the same night as the official opening of the fourth annual baseball tournament. Mayor Schuyler Crawford presented the stadium, and Commissioner Charles Lawrence accepted the honor for his father, the late Robert

> **WICHITA BASEBALL MUSEUM**
>
> **WHAT:** Museum
>
> **WHERE:** 275 S McLean Blvd.
>
> **COST:** Free, Monday–Friday 9 a.m.–5 p.m. when events are not hosted. Call 316-221-8000 to ensure the facility is open and available for tours.
>
> **PRO TIP:** The museum often rotates memorabilia, so repeat visits are recommended.

The Wichita Baseball Heritage wall displays trophies, game merchandise, and uniforms worn by notable players. The original Lawrence-Dumont Stadium replaced the Ackerman Island ballpark in 1934 after it was destroyed by fire.

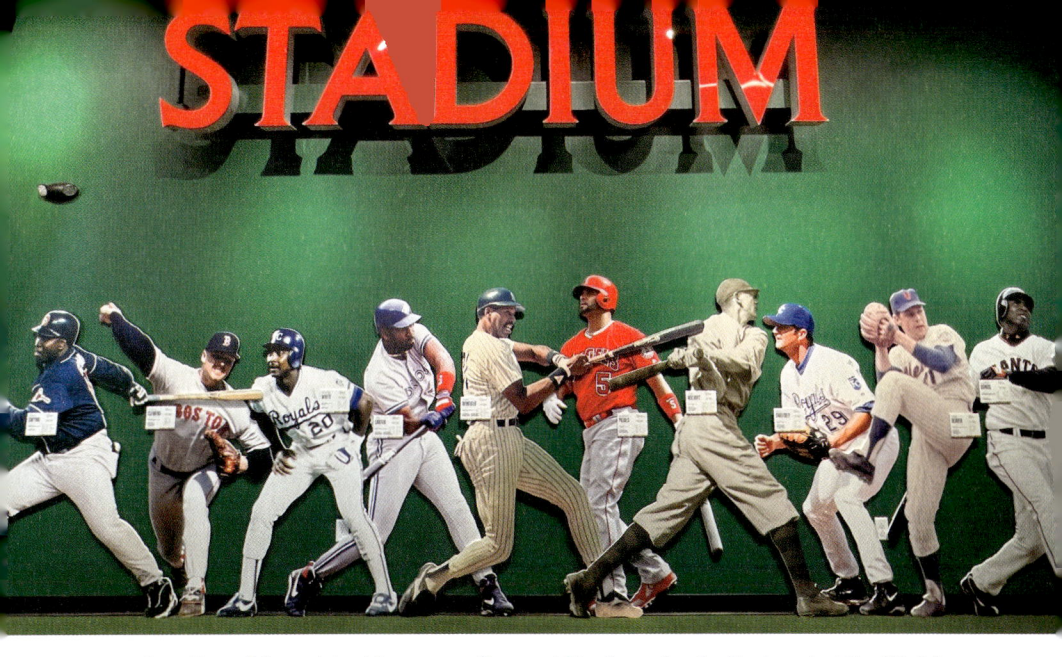

*A section of the original Lawrence-Dumont Stadium sign is displayed at the Wichita Baseball Museum. The stadium replaced the Ackerman Island ballpark in the 1930s, making it a hub for local baseball.*

Lawrence. The price of admission to the game? Spectators paid 40 cents for either grandstand or temporary seats and 25 cents for box seats.

Wichita baseball history is incomplete without acknowledging Ray "Hap" Dumont, who promised to host semi-pro games in the new Lawrence Stadium. Not only did he guarantee $1,000 to bring the racially integrated Bismarck Churchills to play at the stadium in the first NBC Championship, but the team also won in front of large crowds. The museum features original NBC merchandise and a timeline illustrating the historical moments in Wichita's baseball history.

Built in 2020, Riverfront Stadium continues the tradition of making history. The scoreboard was one of the largest in minor league baseball at the time of installation. The Wichita Wind Surge opened its first season at the stadium in April of the following year. When the stadium is full of spectators, 10,000 baseball fans cheer in approval for the Double-A Affiliate team.

# KEEP ON ROCKIN'

**What noisy little bar do locals visit when they want to listen to big sound?**

Since the founding of Kirby's Beer Store in 1972, Wichita State University students, retired faculty, and the city's residents have flocked to the bar for its live music scene and electric atmosphere. It's a sensory overload. The walls are covered in band fliers and stickers. Sports trophies hang upside-down from the ceiling. Do you happen to have a Sharpie® with you? Go ahead and write on the walls in the bathroom. Everyone else does. The bar remains dark, as all its windows are covered in stickers and neon beer signs.

Self-proclaimed as "Wichita's Five Star Dive Bar," the music venue hosts bands of all genres. Because Kirby's doesn't charge a cover fee to listen to live music, the bands are paid in tips from the crowd and free Pabst pints. When a band isn't playing at the drinking establishment, the jukebox kicks out tunes. Pinging sounds can be heard from the bar's pinball machine.

Need to get some fresh air? Head out to the covered patio, where you'll likely find another band playing. Other popular events at the bar include Goth Nite!, Comedy Open Mic, and Quarterball Wednesday, when patrons save 25 cents on pinball games and pizza is served $2.50 off.

---

### KIRBY'S BEER STORE

**WHAT:** Bar

**WHERE:** 3227 E 17th St. N

**COST:** No cover charge

**PRO TIP:** Attending a loud concert? Ask the bartender to sell you a pair of earplugs. They are located in a schooner glass on the bar.

---

Kirby's Beer Store is only 600-square-feet in size.

*Patrons sitting in the few available bar seats are privy to views of random items hanging on the wall. Can you spot the bowling pin? The skateboard?*

Over 300 Google reviews have given the self-proclaimed "premier hole-in-the-wall" bar a near-perfect five-star rating, describing it as a "cool hip venue" and a "pearl among sand."

# CELESTIAL CREATION

**Where can a full moon be viewed 24/7?**

The metal work of Mullinville, Kansas, artist Myron Thomas Liggett, a.k.a. "M. T.", is considered unique, bold, and strikingly curious. How did some of his best artwork end up at Central Standard Brewing, over 150 miles from where it was created?

Central Standard Brewing co-owner Ian Crane visited Greensburg, a town near Mullinville, on a photojournalism assignment while a senior at Wichita State University. The project? To gather stories about Greensburg, which had been almost completely devastated after an EF5 tornado leveled it on May 4, 2007.

During Ian's two-week stay in Greensburg, he made the 10-mile drive to Mullinville to meet Liggett. After befriending him, Ian eventually convinced Liggett to allow him to film a biography about the man and his eccentric roadside art. Like all good friends, they kept in touch over the years. Much later, Ian and his wife, Sumer, made another trek to Liggett's art

## CENTRAL STANDARD BREWING

**WHAT:** Folk art

**WHERE:** 156 S Greenwood St.

**COST:** Drinks $6–$8

**PRO TIP:** If you want to view Liggett's workshop firsthand, the M. T. Liggett Art Environment is open most days in Mullinville, Kansas. The outdoor artwork is on display 24/7.

---

Folk art fans will appreciate M. T. Liggett Art Environment, a museum on the late artist's 20-acre property on the outskirts of Mullinville, Kansas, off US Highway 400. Back buildings remain untouched, including one that houses over 6,000 coffee cups.

*The cartoonish moon by M.T. Liggett is a focal point of Central Standard Brewing's interior design. The artist saw it firsthand when he visited the brewery with his girlfriend.*

complex, where they purchased pieces of his work to bring back to Wichita. With a little convincing, Liggett sold one of his larger and most iconic pieces, the Moon. Today, the celestial creation and a few scrap metal totems adorn the brewery.

On August 17, 2017, Liggett passed away at 86, but people's interest in his art lives on. The folk artist was a provocateur, so it's only natural to wonder why he created roadside sculptures with goofy faces, spinning whirligigs, and oddly shaped animals. And he wasn't afraid to create installations around polarizing political themes, either. Liggett's artwork as a collection often evokes a reaction, which is what the artist wanted. He was known for creating arguments, because he could always take the opposite opinion. Like his conversations with others, his artwork tends to make people think, to wonder why, to challenge one's beliefs, and to try to identify the reason for each piece.

Liggett was a man who liked engaging in conversations, so perhaps his creations should hang in the background as brewerygoers enjoy beer and conversation with friends.

# SAILING SYMBOL

**Why is a replica of a ship sitting in the street during a city festival?**

Is it a boat? Why does it have a cannon? The Wichita Wagonmasters' Windwagon is a massive replica of a ship known for making appearances at the city's largest festivals. Referred to as "the biggest toy in the territory," it is operated by the Wichita RiverFest's Admiral Windwagon Smith each year. The windwagon is the official symbol of the festival.

An architect, Sam Mobley, designed the prairie schooner in 1973 with encouragement from his wife, Margaret. A Disney animated film, *The Saga of Windwagon Smith*, inspired his design. Its design included all of the necessary features of a wind-propelled covered wagon. Sometimes called a sailing wagon, original windwagons were built to skim the Kansas prairie at speeds of up to 40 miles per hour.

Fast-forward to today: the Windwagon continues to appear at the annual Wichita RiverFest. An admiral is nominated annually by the Trail Bosses, past admirals, and Wichita Festivals, Inc.'s board of directors. After he's chosen by the PAWS (Past Admirals Windwagon Smith),

---

**WICHITA WINDWAGON**

**WHAT:** Boat

**WHERE:** Downtown

**COST:** Free

**PRO TIP:** When not used by the Wagonmasters, it is housed at Old Cowtown Museum.

---

The windwagon has traveled outside the city limits. It appeared in the Macy's Thanksgiving Day Parade in New York City in 1975.

*The current ship,* Windwagon II, *makes an appearance at the Wichita River Festival. The names of past Admirals Windwagon Smith are listed on its side.*

he walks under an arch of mops held by The Elite Guard of the Windwagon. Later, the admiral and his court, a.k.a. Prairie Schooner Mates, appear at events like the Sundown Parade to kick off the festival. During other times of the year, it shows up at various events. During the Wagonmasters' Chili Cook-off, a cannon is fired from the wagon, signaling the event's start.

# FRAGRANT FACTORY

**How is it that a historic building has always boasted pungent aromas on the inside?**

One building in town has always been known for its smell. The Spice Merchant sells bulk aromatic spices and gourmet coffee in a historic building on Douglas Avenue. When Albert Alexander Hyde used the same structure to produce mentholatum in the early 1900s, it took on a more medicinal scent.

A former banker turned entrepreneur and real estate investor, A. A. Hyde moved to Kansas and created The Yucca Company with fellow investors in 1889. The company sold shaving cream, perfume, soaps derived from yucca, and, more importantly, a throat-soothing product, Vest Pocket Cough Specific. Intrigued by the use of menthol, Hyde got to work in his home kitchen testing formulas. In 1894, he created mentholatum, an ointment with aromatic vapors used as a topical analgesic rub. People loved using the "Little Nurse for Little Ills."

Renamed The Mentholatum Company, Hyde focused on producing one product in the Wichita factory with a second factory in Buffalo, New York. Hyde knew he needed a large facility to produce the in-demand medicinal product. The total cost to build the one-story structure, complete with a basement at each end, cost $20,000. The *Wichita Daily Beacon* reported in 1909 that the Spanish Mission–style building of concrete and terra cotta was "modern in every respect and is absolutely fireproof." In 1909, the Douglas Avenue and Cleveland Street factory employed 22 people

---

Another building in town, Hyde Elementary, was named after the businessman. He attended its first open house on May 2, 1930. The school now is known as Hyde Leadership and International Magnet.

*Advertisements and jars of mentholatum are displayed in the Wichita-Sedgwick County Historical Museum, including a photo of A. A. Hyde.*

and a staff of seven traveling salesmen.

Considered a generous man, Hyde's financial contributions from the success of his business benefitted the YMCA, The Children's Home, First Presbyterian Church, and many others. Hyde died in 1935 and was laid to rest in Maple Grove Cemetery.

## THE SPICE MERCHANT

**WHAT:** Building

**WHERE:** 1300 E Douglas Ave.

**COST:** Free to tour; products for sale are individually priced.

**PRO TIP:** Want to learn more about Hyde's successful mentholatum business? Tour the Wichita-Sedgwick County's Historical Museum's The Drug Store permanent exhibit and "Wichita—The Magic City" room.

# NO SHIPPING FEES

**What if shipping containers were stacked like building blocks?**

The developers behind Revolutsia, a shipping container mall, were thinking outside the box when they decided to design a shopping mall unlike any other in the city.

The retail plaza is made up of 36 shipping containers of varying lengths, stacked to create a two-story shopping mall with a courtyard at the center. Unlike a standard strip mall, Revolutsia borrows a construction method used in big cities like Tulsa's The Boxyard or Los Angeles's SteelCraft. Repurposed shipping containers are considered not only more cost-effective than traditional construction materials, but they also are sustainable.

At Revolutsia, supporting local businesses is paramount, as each is locally owned and operated. Visitors can expect to purchase goods from various retailers that sell everything from candles to clothes and cupcakes to cocktails. In need of a haircut? The salon or barber shop is ready to book an appointment.

Aside from retail stores, Revolutsia is a place where the community can gather around the

### REVOLUTSIA

**WHAT:** Shopping Mall

**WHERE:** 2721 E Central Ave.

**COST:** Products for sale are individually priced.

**PRO TIP:** Follow Revolutsia's Facebook page to view store and restaurant events listed in one place.

---

Revolutsia is "a fundamental change in the way of thinking about or visualizing something; a change in paradigm."

*The courtyard is the shipping container mall's central focal point, featuring a firepit, swings, and free-to-use hula hoops.*

courtyard fireplace or get together for dinner at one of the eateries. And that's just the point. Revolutsia was built to foster a sense of belonging, where people hang out, shop, and dine in good company.

# UNDER, OVER

**Where can you drive under an airport runway with planes taking off and landing from it?**

One most likely never forgets the time they were driving under a bridge, only to notice that an airplane was simultaneously landing on or taking off from it. The Beechcraft Factory Airport tunnel provides east side drivers access along Central Avenue between Rock and Greenwich roads, a neighborhood hub for aviation activity. Planes departing and arriving from Beech Factory Airport use the runway, so it's common for air traffic to cross above passing motorists who are driving through the tunnel. At night, it provides drivers a unique experience. The Beechcraft neon signs shine bright, and the tunnel lights illuminate the path.

A Wichita company founded in the 1930s, Beechcraft made a name for itself as one of the pioneering companies in the aviation industry. Walter H. Beech and his wife, Olive Ann, aimed to build the "finest aircraft in the world."

The company produced the Beechcraft Model 17 biplane, known as the Staggerwing, and

## BEECH FACTORY AIRPORT RUNWAY

**WHAT:** Tunnel

**WHERE:** Central Ave. between Rock and Greenwich Rds.

**COST:** Free

**PRO TIP:** Access aopa.org and search KBEC to view a satellite image of Beech Factory Airport's runway.

---

Rumor has it that police run radar on Central Ave. on opposite ends of the tunnel, so drivers are cautioned to watch their speeds. Motorcyclists and muscle cars are often heard revving their engines when driving through it.

*A curving road along Central Ave. winds through a tunnel beneath Beechcraft Factory Airport's runway on the city's east side.*

the Beechcraft Bonanza piston, which is the longest continually produced aircraft in the world. In addition, the company is known for its turboprops, including the King Air.

    Depending on the day, drivers passing through the tunnel under the Beech Factory Airport runway may notice one of these planes or others passing overhead.

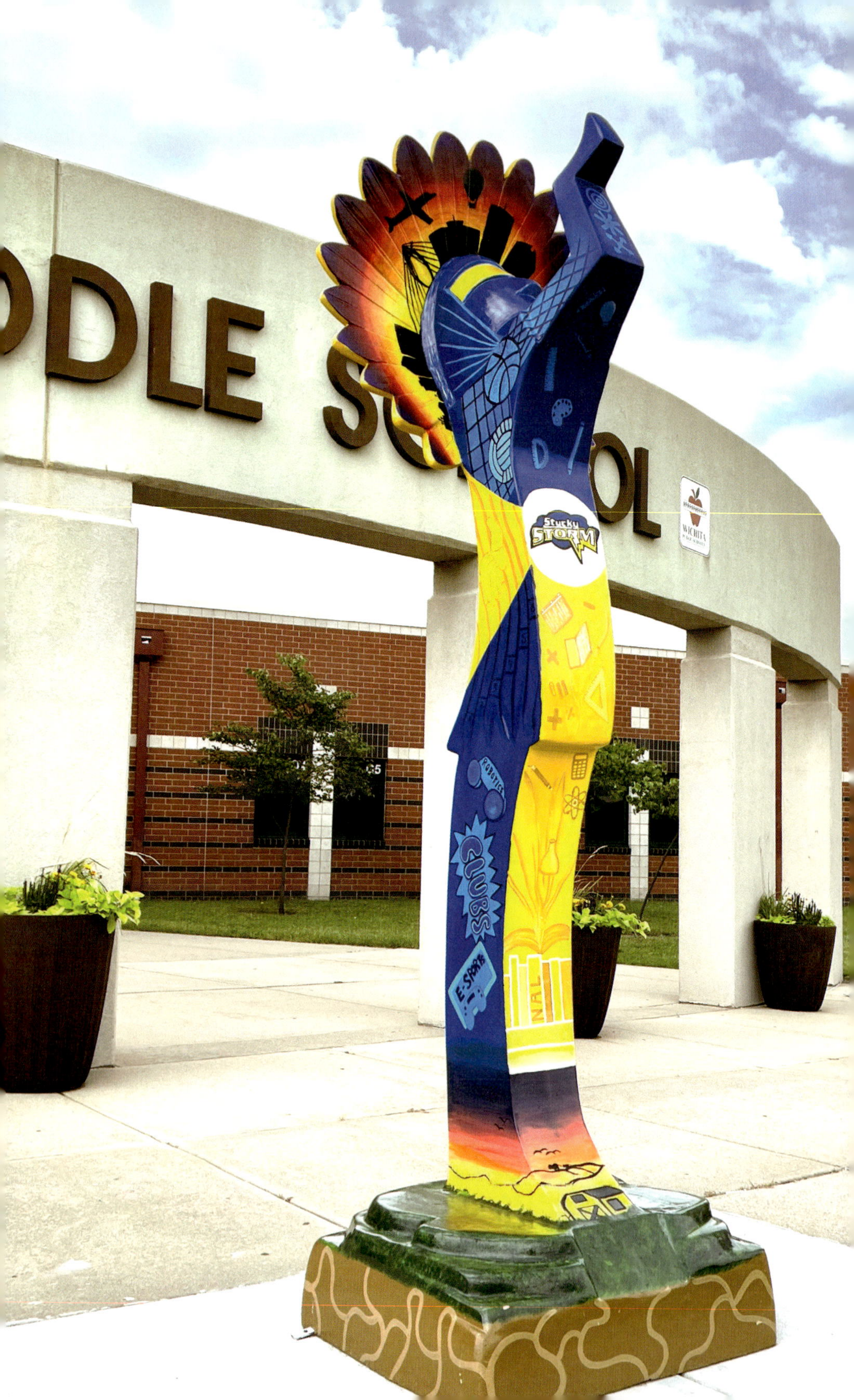
Stucky
STORM
CLUBS

# SOURCES

**Below-Ground Goblin:**
Travel Translator: A Guide to the Local Language in Wichita, "The Troll," Visit Wichita, visitwichita.com, March 29, 2021
Wichita's Riverside Parks by James E. Mason, Arcadia Publishing, 2011
"The Wichita Troll" by Chris Clemons, Atlas Obscura, atlasobscura.com, 2022

**Isle of Interest:**
"Picnic Sunday at Ackerman Island," the *Wichita Beacon*, July 8, 1892
"Roller Coaster is Ready: Wonderland Park Will Be Open Saturday Afternoon," the *Wichita Eagle*, Oct. 26, 1905
"How The Old Sand-Bar In Wichita, Now Vanishing, Grew To Be An Island," the *Wichita Beacon*, Dec. 8, 1933
"Dream of 'Never-Never' Land on Ackerman Island Realized," the *Wichita Sunday Eagle*, Jan. 10, 1937
Episode 611 by Jim Grade, *Positively Kansas*, PBS Kansas, 2022

**Traditions Reign Supreme:**
"History of North High School," Wichita North High School, usd259.org, 2023
Tower Yearbook, North High School, 1930
Tower Yearbook, North High School, 1938

**City Founder:**
"Places of Repose: Early Cemeteries of Wichita" by Eric Cale, The Maple Grove Cemetery, maplegrovecemetery.org, 2018
"The History of Kansas Railroads," Kansas Department of Transportation, ksdot.org, 2023
"James R. Mead," Towanda Area Historical Museum, storyoftowanda.org, 2023
'Western Trails,' James R. Mead: Trader and Townbuilder Exhibit, Wichita State Special Collections, 2023

**Steel Sculpture:**
"Sculpture Portrays Heritage," the *Wichita Eagle*, May 12, 1974
"Known for his *Keeper of the Plains*, Blackbear Bosin was a prolific artist," KSN News, ksn.com, Oct. 17, 2019
"Blackbear Bosin," Kansas Historical Society, kshs.org, May 2006

**Rowdy Route:**
"Douglas Avenue Bridge," PocketSights Tour Guide, Google Play, 2023
"Wild West Delano," PocketSights Tour Guide, Google Play, 2023
"Delano's Colorful History," Historic Delano, historicdelano.com, 2023

**Ever the Eccentric:**
Site visit

**Preserved Plane:**
AF-1, Yard Store, af1.yardstore.com, 2023
Beech Aircraft Company, Kansas Historical Society, kshs.org, October 2022

**Mood Flags:**
"'Oh, Happy Day' flag signaled a good day at the office for Beech aircraft executive," the *Wichita Eagle*, Feb. 15, 2018
"Olive Ann Beech: Queen of the Aircraft Industry," Archbridge Institute, May 15, 2018

171

"Olive Ann Beech: the Woman from Waverly Who Changed Aviation History," Kansas Public Radio, June 12, 2019

"Olive Ann Mellor Beech," Kansas Historical Society, kshs.org, August 2002

**Tree Tunnel:**
"Chisholm Creek Park," Great Plains Nature Center, gpnc.org, 2017

**Station Sign:**
"The Union Station and the Elevated Tracks in Tabloid," the *Wichita Beacon*, March 6, 1914

"Wichita's Big Station Is to Be the Last of a Noble Race," the *Wichita Beacon*, March 7, 1914

**Gas Station Grub:**
"History" Pumphouse, pumphousewichita.com, 2023

**Saved By the Bell:**
"Through The Years With McCormick School 1890-1975," McCormick School, 1976

"McCormick Bellringer," McCormick School Museum, mccormickschoolmuseum.com, 2018

**Whistle-Stop Wonder:**
"Wichita Toy Train Museum: Operated by Wichita Toy Train Club," Wichita Toy Train Museum, wichitatoytrainmuseum.org, 2023

**Stellar Stone:**
"Eye on the Solstice," the *Wichita Eagle*, June 18, 2004

"A glowing start of summer." the *Wichita Eagle*, June 22, 2006

"Mural adds 'Magic' to design district," the *Wichita Eagle*, June 28, 2014

**Sci-Fi Sculpture:**
"Randy Regier, *Celestial Mechanic*, 2019," Ulrich Museum of Art, YouTube, 2019

"World Art Day: 15 little known facts about sculptures on your campus," Wichita State University, April 15, 2022

**Go Glazy:**
The Donut Whole, facebook.com/thedonutwhole, 2023

**Path Forward:**
"Wizard of Oz in Wichita," 360Wichita, 360Wichita.com, Jan. 17, 2017

**Fit for Royalty:**
"Midtown Structures Largely from 1800s," the *Wichita Eagle* and *Beacon*, Sept. 24, 1978

"1155 N. River Blvd," Zillow, zillow.com, Jan. 25, 2023

**Colorful Creation:**
"A Touch of Glass," the *Wichita Eagle*, April 20, 2003

"Museum to take glass ceiling apart for dusting," the *Wichita Eagle*, March 4, 2012

**Significant Sign:**
"Chisholm Trail and The Birth of Wichita: History on the Hoof," Wichita Public Library Special Collections Storage, Sept. 14, 2016

"The Chisholm Trail in Wichita, Kansas," Kansas Historical Society, kshs.org, 2017

"The Chisholm Trail," Kansas Historical Society, kshs.org, 1936

"Driving the Herd: Jesse Chisholm & The Chisholm Trail," Visit Wichita, visitwichita.com, July 25, 2017

"Chisholm Trail Jubilee Official Program, Wichita - Chisholm Trail

Historical Story," Ross McLaury Taylor, 1958
"Delano's Colorful History" Historic Delano, historicdelano.com, 2019

**Ornate Office:**
"Mr. Carey On His Policy," the Wichita Weekly Beacon, April 10, 1891
"John B. Carey Dead," the *Weekly Eagle*, Nov. 24, 1899

**Designed to Shine:**
"Artist Aware Work Seen in 2 Ways," the *Wichita Eagle*, Dec. 11, 1984
"John Kearney's 'Horse' and Other Chrome Bumper Sculptures," the *Wichita Eagle*, June 4, 1995
"Kearney, John Walter," the *Chicago Tribune*, August 17, 2014
"World Art Day: 15 little known facts about sculptures on your campus," WSU News, April 15, 2022
"Chrome Bumper Sculptures," Visit Wichita, visitwichita.com, 2023

**Lady Liberty:**
"Statue of Liberty Replicated Dedicated as U.N. Week Ends," the *Wichita Eagle*, Oct. 29, 1951
"Commemorating the Boy Scouts of America's 40th Anniversary" Liberty Sisters, libertysisters.com, 2023

**Better in Bronze:**
"Douglas Dream," the *Wichita Eagle*, Aug. 11, 1996
"Douglas Avenue Streetscape," Georgia Gerber, georgiagerber.com, 2022

**Magnificent Murals:**
"Avenue Art Days will end with one final mural, party," the *Wichita Eagle*, August 21, 2022

**The First Buffalo Bill:**
"William Mathewson Dead; He Expired Asleep In Chair," the *Wichita Eagle*, March 21, 1916
"Pioneers Pay Last Tributes," the *Wichita Eagle*, March 24, 1916
"William E. Mathewson–The Other Buffalo Bill," Legends of America, legendsofamerica.com, 2023
"Plainsman, Merchant, Indian Scout," Wichita-Sedgwick County Historical Museum, 2023
"William Mathewson," Find a Grave, findagrave.com, 2023

**Totally Tiki:**
"Reclaiming the Tiki Bar," the *New York Times*, Dec. 27, 2020

**Strumming Steel:**
"Origin of the Electric Guitar," Internet Archive, archive.org, October 13, 2018
"The History of the Electric Guitar," Humanities Kansas, Dec. 1, 2020
"Ro-Pat-In's First Electric Spanish: Granddaddy to the Stars!" *Vintage Guitar Magazine*, 2008

**Frontline Fighters:**
"House of TANK Museum," House of Tank, Facebook, 2023

**On The Range:**
"The Story of Wichita's First Dwelling" the *Wichita Eagle*, April 23, 1910
"Wichita, A Pictorial History" by Kay Kirkman, Donning Company, 1981
"Wichita's Riverside Parks" by James E. Mason, Arcadia Publishing, 2011
"The Munger House – 2 steps, narrow doorway" by Old Cowtown Museum, PocketSights Travel Guide, pocketsights.com, 2023

**173**

**Tiny Towns:**
"*Kansas in Miniature*," the *Journal of American History*, Vol. 87, Issue 3, December 2000
"*Kansas in Miniature*: Virtual Tour," Exploration Place, YouTube, June 11, 2020

**Movie Legend:**
"McDaniel opened doors," the *Wichita Eagle*, Nov. 7, 1991
"Famous Kansan: Hattie McDaniel," Read Kansas! Kansas Historical Society, 2006
"'Dignity and Grace': New Historical Marker Showcases The Life, Legacy of Hattie McDaniel," KMUW, March 31, 2021
"39c Hattie McDaniel single," Smithsonian National Postal Museum, postalmuseum.si.edu, 2022

**Daring Design:**
"Frank Lloyd Wright's Genius Demonstrated," the *Wichita Eagle*, July 19, 1964
"Regents, Faculty Dedicate Corbin Education Center," the *Wichita Eagle*, June 29, 1964
"Corbin Education Center," Wichita State University, www.wichita.edu, 2022

**Confidential Cocktails:**
"The License System and Joints," *Western Methodist*, April 10, 1890
"Dockum meant pharmacy," the *Wichita Eagle*, Oct. 18, 1990
"Dockum Apothecary Speakeasy," WDM Architects, wdmarchitects.com, 2023

**Made in Wichita:**
"The Jones Six," advertisement, the *Wichita Eagle*, April 29, 1915
"The 1916 Jones VI Automobile," exhibit, Wichita-Sedgwick County Historical Museum, wichitahistory.org, 2022

**Alley Art:**
"Gallery Alley Reopening 2021," Envision, envisionus.com, July 7, 2021
"Downtown Wichita's Gallery Alley wins national placemaking award," Wichita Business Journal, Oct. 7, 2022
"Gallery Alley," Downtown Wichita, downtownwichita.org, 2023

**Grain Elevator Gallery:**
"To Paint A Mural: Horizontes Project Helps North Wichitan See in Color," KMUW, kmuw.org, Jan. 25, 2019
"GLeo Paints '*The Original Dream*' in Kansas," Brooklyn Street Art, brooklynstreetart.com, Jan. 28, 2019
"*El Sueno Original*," Horizontes Project, horizontes-project.com. 2022

**Madwoman Makes Mischief:**
"Chisholm Trail and The Birth of Wichita: History on the Hoof," Wichita Public Library Special Collections Storage, Sept. 14, 2016
"Carry Nation," Encyclopedia Britannica, britannica.com, Nov. 21 2022
"Carry Nation House Museum," Medicine Lodge Stockade Museum, medicinelodgestockade.org, 2022
"Document for December 5th: Presidential Proclamation 2065 of December 5, 1933, in which President Franklin D. Roosevelt announces the Repeal of Prohibition," National Archives, archives.gov, 2023

"Speakeasies of the Prohibition Era," Legends of America, legenddsofamerican.com, 2023

**Merry-Go-Round Memories:**
"Joyland: Reliving the Memories," PBS Kansas, pbs.org, 2019
"The Carousel Project," Botanica, botanica.org, 2023

**Spirits Among Us:**
"History of the Building," Kansas Aviation Museum, kansasaviationmuseum.org, 2023

**Baseball Brilliance:**
"League 42 paying tribute to Jackie Robinson with statue," the *Wichita Eagle*, April 1, 2021
"Jackie Robinson Biography," Jackie Robinson, jackierobinson.com, 2022
"Installations: McAdams Park," Jason Parson, Sculptor, parsonssculpture.com, 2023

**Somewhere Over the Rainbow:**
"Newton Publisher Dies Wednesday Morning," *Mennonite Weekly Review*, Jan. 29, 1930
"Dedicate Bridge Here Tonight," the *Wichita Beacon*, July 22, 1931
"James Barney Marsh," Kansapedia, Kansas Historical Society, kshs.org, May 2011
"John Mack Bridge, Wichita," Kansas Sampler Foundation, kansassampler.org, 2023
"Mack, John," Kansas Press Association Hall of Fame, kspress.com, 2023

**Twisted Tree Limbs:**
"Chisholm Creek Park" Great Plains Nature Center, gpnc.org, 2017

**Moment in Time:**
"James M. Davis," the *Wichita Eagle*, Jan. 18, 1923
"Davis Administration Building," Friends University, friends.edu, 2023

**Tirelessly Standing:**
"The Secret Plot of the Muffler Man," Roadside America, roadsideamerica.com, 2023
"The Story of Muffler Men and other Roadside Giants," It's A Southern Thing, southernthing.com, Nov. 17, 2018
"Muffler Men," International Fiberglass, internationalfiberglassco.com, 2023

**Coffin Curiosity:**
"Antiquities," public auction listing, New York Galleries of Sotheby Parke Bernet, Inc., May 4, 1973
"RIP: On Art and Mourning," Norton Simon Museum, nortonsimon.org, June 9, 2017
"Deities in Ancient Egypt – Nut," Rosicrucian Egyptian Museum, egyptianmuseum.org, 2023

**Bird Characters:**
"Miró Mural Going Up on WSU Campus," the *Wichita Eagle*, Sept. 15, 1978

**Gnome Sweet Gnome:**
"The History of Gnomes – Gnomania," The Curious Historian, curioushistorian.com, 2019
"Our Story," Hopping Gnome Brewery, hoppinggnome.com, 2023

**Keen on History:**
"Wichita Warehouse and Jobbers District," National Register of Historic Places, May 27, 2015

"Hotel at Old Town: Our Historical Wichita Old Town Building Was Once a Keen Kutter Warehouse," Hotel at Old Town, hotelatoldtown.com, 2023

**Peaceful Plaza:**
"Indian Serene in Kiva," the *Wichita Eagle*, Oct. 7, 1973
"When your friend is blind you do what you can–even if you're a duck," the *Wichita Eagle*, May 11, 2017

**The Sky's the Limit:**
"A Bold Expansion in Downtown Wichita," Fidelity Bank, FidelityBank.com, May 7, 2019

**Standing Proudly:**
"Sculpture Portrays Heritage," the *Wichita Eagle*, May 12, 1974
"Known for his *Keeper of the Plains*, Blackbear Bosin was a prolific artist," KSN News, ksn.com, Oct. 17, 2019
"Blackbear Bosin," Kansas Historical Society, kshs.org, May 2006

**Warbird Wonder:**
"What's up, 'Doc?': Restoration of B-29 WWII bomber a remarkable journey," Spectrum News 1, spectrumnews1.com, July 26, 2022
"The B-29 Doc Story," B-29 Doc Hangar, Education, & Visitors Center, b29doc.com, 2023

**A Sew-phisticated Place:**
"Chapman-Noble House," National Register of Historic Places Registration Form, National Park Service National Register Digital Assets, Sept. 20, 2006
"Now You Know: Who Was William Sternberg?" the *Wichita Eagle*, May 31, 2008

**Small Screen:**
"PBS Kansas moving into new, expanded home," the *Wichita Eagle*, April 4, 2022
"Bonavia Foundation PBS Kansas Museum," PBS Kansas, kpts.org, 2023

**Back Alley Artwork:**
"Downtown Wichita Launches Alley Doors Project," press release, Downtown Wichita, downtownwichita.org, Nov. 5, 2020
"Discover Alley Doors," Downtown Wichita, downtownwichita.org, 2023

**Antique Artillery:**
"Cannon Mounted Today: Old Spanish Gun Is to be Places in Riverside Park," the *Weekly Eagle*, Jan. 25, 1901
"Frederick Funston," National Park Service, nps.gov, Aug. 12, 2019
"Complete Details of Unveiling Service at Spanish War Statue," the *Wichita Eagle*, May 23, 1926
"Rare, royal, restored: Spanish-American war bronze revealed," the *Wichita Eagle*, Sept. 22, 2007
"Spanish-American War Memorial," The Historical Marker Database, hmdb.org, 2023

**Creative Complex:**
"The Art Park," The Art Park, theartparkwichita.com, 2023

**Work of Art:**
"Commerce St. Art District Light Sculptures," Fisch Haus, fischhaus.com, Oct. 28, 2016
"From rusty tracks to high-tech sculpture," the *Wichita Eagle*, August 27, 2017
"Kent Thomas Williams" Fisch Haus, fischhaus.com, 2022

"*Railgrass*" IC in the ICT, icintheict.com, 2023

### Colorful Craftsmanship:
"Lao Buddhists building colorful monks' quarters," the *Wichita Eagle*, Oct. 11, 2020

"Buddhism," National Geographic, education.nationalgeographic.org, 2023

### From the Ashes:
"Standing Proudly On The Hill," Wichita State University, Monument Inscription, 1973

A History of Fairmount College by John Rydjord, The Regents Press of Kansas, 1977

"Morrison Library," The Historical Marker Database, www.hmdb.org, July 7, 2022

"The Evolution of the University Libraries," University Libraries, libraries.wichita.edu, Sept. 12, 2022

"Alma Mater Spirit Squad - Traditions," Wichita State University, goshockers.com, 2023

"Carnegie Columns," Explore Wichita State Historical Tour, map.concept3d.com, 2023

### Open-Faced Fun:
"About Us," City Bites, citybites.net, 2023

### Perfected Pizza:
Kansas Curiosities: Third Edition by Pam Grout, Globe Pequot Press, 2019

"Pizza Hut Museum," Wichita State University, wichita.edu, 2023

### Gas Lamp Gridiron:
"Night Football Not a Success: Fairmount Winds From Cooper by 24-0," the *Wichita Beacon*, Oct. 7, 1905

### Rainbow Residences:
Site visit

### IPA in an Igloo:
"Welcome To Our Garden Igloos!" Nortons Brewing Company, nortonsbrewing.com, 2023

### Historic Hideaway:
"'The *Boy and the Boot*,' Wichita's Famous Statue is Being Repaired," the *Wichita Eagle*, August 8, 1921

"Pioneer Spirit Moved Sculptor to Create Nude," the *Wichita Eagle and Beacon*, April 4, 1976

### Monument Masterpiece:
"White Dove As A Symbol of Peace: Thousands Applaud As Monument Is Unveiled," the *Wichita Beacon*, June 14, 1913

"Soldiers and Sailors Civil War Monument," registration form, National Register of Historic Places, Sept. 30, 1998

"Soldiers And Sailors Monument Returns: Back where it belongs," the *Wichita Eagle*, Nov. 10, 2021

"Soldiers and Sailor's Monument," Art Inventories Catalog, Smithsonian Institution Research Information System, 2023

### Tucked-Away Park:
"First Elected Officers of City of Eastborough," the *Wichita Eagle*, June 16, 1937

"Frank L. Dunn Is Named As Mayor Of Eastborough," the *Wichita Eagle*, June 16, 1937

"Welcome To The City of Eastborough," City of Eastborough, eastborough-ks.gov, 2022

### Stone Structure:
"Proudfoot & Bird," Kansas Historical Society, kshs.org, Jan. 2013

"Wichita's Most Beautiful Building," The Scottish Rite, wichitascottishrite.org, 2023

**Animal Art:**
"Sedgwick County Art Walk," sedgwickcountyartwalk.com, 2021

**City's Largest Cigar:**
"A Brief History of the Cigar Industry," Cigar Aficionado, Sept/Oct. 2012
Mort's, mortswichita.com, 2023

**Victorious Voyage:**
"Three T's bring payoff for Koch's America3," the *Wichita Eagle*, May 17, 1992
"William 'Bill' Ingraham Koch" by Gary Jobson, National Sailing Hall of Fame, nshof.org, 2023

**Beyond the Books:**
"The Brass Taproom at Sidepockets," thebrasstaproom.com, 2023

**Play Ball:**
"Baseball Meet Expected to Draw 50,000 Here," the *Wichita Eagle*, July 29, 1934
"Sisler Will Pitch First Ball in Stadium Opener Tonight," the *Wichita Eagle*, August 3, 1934
"The Wichita Baseball Museum," wichitabaseballmuseum.com, 2023

**Keep On Rockin':**
"Kirby's Beer Store," kirbysbeerstore.com, 2023

**Celestial Creation:**
"M.T. Liggett Art Environment," mtliggettartenvironment.org, 2021

**Sailing Symbol:**
"Windwagon a pioneer's dream," the *Wichita Eagle*, May 3, 1976
Windwagon's Designer Will Proudly Take Helm," the *Wichita Eagle*, May 7, 1984
"Windwagons," Kansas Historical Society, kshs.org, April 2013
"About the Wichita Wagonmasters," Wichita Wagonmasters, wagonmasters.org, 2022

**Fragrant Factory:**
"The New Home of The Mentholatum Company," the *Wichita Daily Beacon*, Aug. 19, 1909
"The Quartet of Hydes," the *Wichita Weekly Eagle*, Dec. 9, 1909
"Albert Alexander Hyde," Kansas Historical Society, kshs.org, May 2013
"About Hyde," Hyde Leadership and International Explorations Magnet, usd259.org, 2023

**No Shipping Fees:**
"About," Revolutsia, revolutsia.com, 2023

**Under, Over:**
"Beechcraft: A History," Textron Aviation, txtav.com, 2023

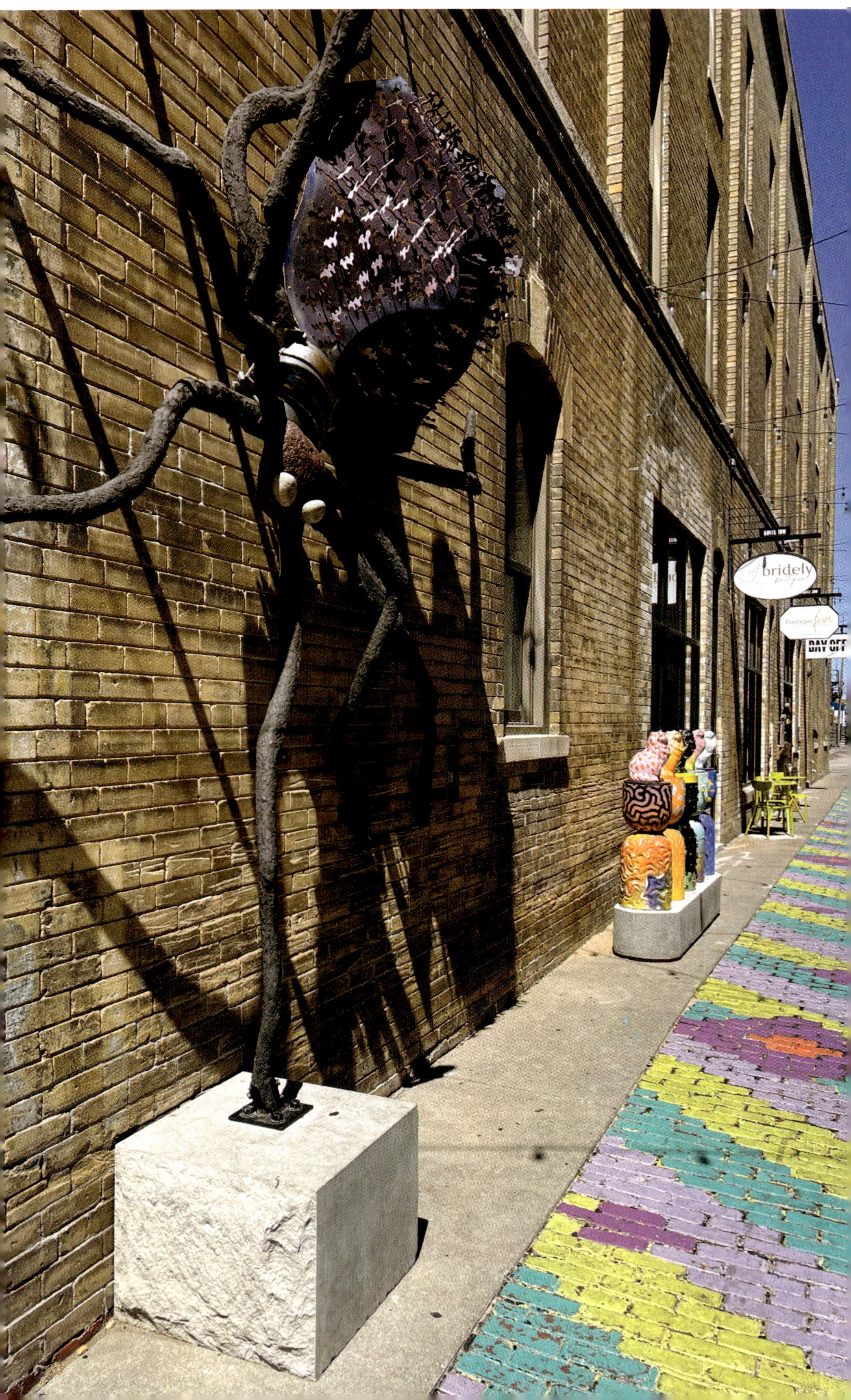
bridely
DAY OFF

# INDEX

20th Kansas Infantry Regiment, 121
1906 Lounge, The, 103
Abilene, 44
Ackerman Island, 6, 7, 156, 157
Ackerman, Joseph, 6
Advanced Learning Library, 108
Agather, Victor N., 111
Air Capital of the World, 18, 102, 110
Air Force One, 18, 19
Allen House, 70
Alley Doors Project, 116, 117
Alteration Shoppe, The, 112
Ambassador Hotel, 73
Ambassador of the Plains, The, 44
*America3*, 152
American Civil War, 96, 97, 142
American Giants, 94
America's Cup, 152
*Ancient Egypt*, 96, 97
Ande Hall, 76
Army Air Corps, 18
Art Park, The, 122, 123
Art Walk, The, 148, 149
Association Park, 134
Atwood, Stephen, 124
Atwood Studio, 124
Avenue Art Days, 54, 55
B-29 Doc Hangar, Education, & Visitors Center, 110, 111
Babb, W. J., 25
*Barefoot Businessman*, 52
Barney, James, 88
Beachner Grain Elevator, 78, 79
Beauchamp, George, 60
Beech Aircraft Corporation, 18
Beech Factory Airport, 168, 169
Beech, Olive Ann, 20, 21, 171
Beech, Walter H., 18, 20, 21, 102, 168
Beechcraft, 168, 169
Bender, John, 132
Bergen, Richard, 140
*Beulah Show, The*, 68
Big Arkansas River, 88
Bigfoot, 67
Bismarck Churchills, 157
Boats and Bikes, 153
Boeing, 12, 110
Bonavia Foundation, 114
Bosin, Francis "Blackbear", 12, 13
Botanica, 5, 82, 83

Boxyard, The, 166
Boy Scouts of America, 50
Brass Taproom, The, 154
Brewer, Gage, 60, 61
Brooklyn Dodgers, 86
Brown's Tire and Custom Wheel Center, 94, 95
Buffalo Bill, 56, 57
Byers, Heather, 55
California, 47, 69, 94, 96, 97, 136
Callen, Kelly, 128
Campbell Castle, 40, 41
Campbell, Colonel Burton Harvey, 40
Cape Cod, 48
Carey Hotel, The, 80, 81
Carey House, The, 46
Carey, John B., 46
Carey Lumber Company, The, 47
Carnegie Library, 128, 140
Carney, Beverly, 133
Carney, Frank, 132
Castle Inn Riverside, 40, 113
*Celestial Mechanic*, 34
Central Riverside Park, 32, 33, 120, 121
Central Standard Brewing, 160
Chapman-Noble House, 112
Chief Satanta, 56
Chihuly, Dale, 42, 43
Children's Home, The, 165
Children's Museum of Wichita, 31
Chisholm Creek Park, 22
Chisholm, Jesse, 44, 56
Chisholm Trail, 14, 15, 44, 45, 48, 49
Churn and Burn, 36
City Bites, 130, 131
City Hall, 46, 47, 140
City of Eastborough, 144
Civil War, 96, 97, 142, 143
*Cleopatra at the Bath*, 80
Clifton Square, 137
Cochener-Garvey Children's Education & Discovery Center, 114
Coffeyville, 49
Coleman Company, The, 118, 134
College Hill Park, 136
*Colorblind Sunset*, 55
Comanche, 12, 44
Comet A34, 62
Commerce Art District, 125
Conrad, Katherine, 39
Corbett, Terry, 33, 148
Corbin Education Center, 70, 71
Corbin, Harry F., 70
Cottonwood Trail, 23

Crane, Ian, 160
Crane, Sumer, 161
Crawford, Schuyler, 156
Crown Uptown, 137
Damm Music Center, 61
Dannar-Garcia, Leah, 106
Davis Administration Building, 92, 93
Davis, James M., 92
*Dear Wichita, Take Care & Dream Big*, 55
DeBoer, Jack, 102
Delano BBQ, 13
DeVore, Dick, 52
Diver Studio, 4
Dockum, 52, 72, 73
Dockum, Harry, 72
Dodge City, 14
Donut Whole, The, 36
Dougherty, Patrick, 90
Douglas Avenue Bridge, 7, 15, 44
Douglas Avenue Streetscape, 52, 53
Douglas Design District, 54, 137
Downtown Wichita, 12, 30, 52, 58, 76, 104, 106, 116, 117
Dumont, Ray "Hap", 157
Dunn, Frank L., 144
Eastborough Park, 145
East High School, 50, 51
Eaton Place, 46, 47, 52, 80, 81
Eckels, Carla, 128
Eck Stadium, 133
Edmonton, Kathleen, 128
Eftekhar, Alex, 118, 119
Egyptian Room, The, 146
Elgin, 14
Ellsworth County, 66
Elvis, 58
Ernatt, Connie, 4
Eunice Sterling Chapter of the Daughters of the American Revolution, 65
Exploration Place, 7, 66, 67, 109
Fairmount College, 128, 129
Fidelity Bank, 106, 107, 140
Finnegan & Wood, 60
First Friday, 116
First Mile Cantine, 106
First Presbyterian Church, 165
Fisch Haus, 124
Flint Hills, 149
Ford, Henry, 74
Friends University, 92, 93, 146
Funston, Frederick, 12
Galena, 94
Gallery Alley, 76

Garfield University, 92, 146
Garvey Center, 104, 105
Garvey Ducks, 104, 105
Garvey Garage, 104
Garvey, Olive W., 104
Geary, 45
Gerber, Georgia, 52
Gill's Funeral Home, 57
GLeo, 78
Glinda the Good Witch, 38
Gold Star Mothers, 121
Gott, Henry V., 50
*Grandfather's Horse*, 49
Great Plains Transportation Museum, 25
Greensburg, 160
Greiffenstein, William, 56
Griswold, John, 97
Grow, 106
Guinness World Record, 78
Gypsum Hills, 66
Hall, Ande, 76
Harmon, Sara Joy, 7
Harrison, Colonel J. N., 143
Heritage Square Park, 140, 141
Hibbard, Frederick Cleveland, 142
Highland Cemetery, 56, 57
Historic Delano District, 14, 15, 45, 49
Historic Preservation Board, 44
Historic Wichita, Inc., 65
Hopping Gnome Brewing Company, 37, 100, 175
Horizontes Project, 78, 79
House of Tank, 62, 63
Hutchinson, 40
Hyde, A. A., 11, 164, 165
Hyde Elementary, 164
Hyde Leadership and International Magnet, 164
*Il Moro di Venezia*, 152
Industrial Revolution, 112
International Downtown Association, 77
International Fiberglass Company, 94
INTRUST Bank Arena, 125
Irby-Gilliland Company, 134
Island Park, 6
Japan, 110
*Jayhawk, The*, 152, 153
Jewell, Ruth, 9
John Mack Bridge, 88, 89
Jones Auto Exchange, 74
Jones, John, 74
Jones Motor Car Company, The, 74

**181**

Joyland Amusement Park, 36, 37, 82
Judge Sluss, 57
Junior League of Wichita, 140
Jury Eye Care, 116, 117
Kansas Academy of Science, 10
Kansas African American Museum, The, 69
Kansas Aviation Museum, 20, 21, 84, 85
Kansas Coliseum, 49
Kansas Department of Commerce, 106
Kansas Gas and Electric, 12
Kansas High Wheel Society, 118
*Kansas in Miniature*, 66, 67
Kansas Public Radio, 20
Kansas Sports Hall of Fame, 153
Kansas State Historical Society, 10
Kansas United Spanish War Veterans, 44
Kearney, John Walter, 48
Keen Kutter, 102, 103
*Keeper of the Plains*, 4, 12, 13, 108, 137, 171, 176
Keepers on Parade, 103, 108, 137
Kelcy's Dance Studio, 122
Kentucky, 116
Kernodle, Lindsey, 55
Khicha Carousel, 82
King, Freddie, 60
Kiowa, 12, 44, 56
Kirby's Beer Store, 158
Kiva Plaza, 104, 105
Knight Foundation, 76, 116
Koch, Bill, 152
Laidlaw, Florence, 28
Lao Buddhist Associates of Kansas, 126, 127
Lattin, Stacy, 100
Lawrence, Charles, 156
Lawrence-Dumont Stadium, 156, 157
Lawrence, Robert, 156
League 42, 86, 87
Leopard 1A5, 62
*Les Grandes Bresses*, 76
Liggett, M. T., 160–161
Lindsey Kernodle & Friends, 55
Little Arkansas River, 9, 41, 44, 64
*Looking to the Future*, 55
Los Angeles, 69, 166
Lutz, Bob, 86
Lytton's Appliance Showroom, 55
M. T. Liggett Art Environment, 160
Mack, John C., 88
Maize South High School, 49

Mammoth Monster, 82
Manning, John, 60
Maple Grove Cemetery, 11, 165
Marcus Welcome Center, 133
Mark Arts, 90, 91
Martin H. Bush Outdoor Sculpture Collection, 34
Mason, Sontia Levy, 54
Masons, 146
Mathewson, William, 56, 57
Mathews, Kenneth W. 121
Mazzolini, Tony, 111
McAdams Park, 86
McCormick Elementary School, 28
McCormick, John, 28
McDaniel, Hattie, 68, 69
McJimsey, Pat, 60
McKnight Arts Center, 128
McLean Boulevard, 44
*Mead Crossing the Arkansas*, 55
Mead, J. R., 55, 56
Medicine Lodge, 80
Mellor, Babs, 81
Memorial Hall, 143
Mentholatum Company, The, 164, 165
Mid-America All-Indian Museum, 12
Midget Monster, 82
Miller, Mike, 76
Minisa Bridge, 9
Minjarez, Armando, 78
Miró, Joan, 98
Mobley, Margaret, 162
Mobley, Sam, 162
Model 17, 18, 168
Mojave Desert, 111
Monarch, The, 14
Monart School of Art, 123
Monrovians, 156
Montemurro, Tom, 104
Morrison, Nathan J., 128, 129
Mort's Martini and Cigar Bar, 150
Mountain Dew, 16
Muffler Man, 94, 95
Mullinville, 160
Munger, D. S., 64, 65, 142
Munger House, 64, 65
Munger, Julia P., 142
Munger, Mary E., 64
Munger Post Office, 64
Murillo, Steve, 33, 103
Museum of World Treasures, 96, 97
Mushroom Rock, 66
*Music's Magic*, 32
Nation, Carry, 46

National Baseball Congress, 156
National Geographic, 126
National Register of Historic Places, 65, 80, 88, 93, 112, 142, 147
National Sailing Hall of Fame, 152
Newman, Allen George III, 121
Nellis, Philip, 55
Northeast Magnet High School, 108
North High School, 1, 8
Nortons Brewing Company, 138
NuWay, 67
O. J. Watson Park, 38
Oklahoma, 12, 45, 60, 90, 130
Old Cowtown Museum, 64, 65, 142, 162
Old Mill Tasty Shop, 76
Old Sedgwick County Courthouse, 142
Old Town, 24, 27, 102, 103, 108, 150
Old Town Cigars, 150
Old Town Garage, 27
Omaha, 48
Original Dream, The, 78, 79
Osage, 44
Pacific Coast Conference, 87
Palace of the Plains, The, 74
Parsons, John, 86, 87
PBS Kansas, 114, 115
Pendergrass, Gary, 16, 17
*Persian Seaform Installation*, 42, 43
*Personnages Oiseaux*, 98, 99
Piccadilly, 118
Pirtle, John, 116, 117
Pitt, Brad, 63
Pizza Hut, 132, 133
Pizza Hut Museum, 132, 133
Planeview, 67
Pratt, Terri, 84
Prohibition Era, 72, 80, 81, 154
Proudfoot and Bird, 28, 146
Pumphouse, The, 26, 27
*Railgrass*, 124, 125
Rainbow Row, 136, 137
Regier, Randy, 34
Republic of Texas, 44
Revard, Carter, 125
Reverie Roasters, 37
Revolutsia, 166, 167
RISE Farms, 106, 107
Riverfront Stadium, 156, 157
Ro-Pat-In "Electro" Guitar Spanish Model, 61
Robinson, Jackie, 86, 87
Roosevelt, Franklin D., 81
Roosevelt Middle School, 51

Ross, Finlay, 6, 120, 140
Route 66, 94
Ruffin Building, 48, 49
Running of the Doves, 14
Rupe, Tobin, 148
Russell, Leon, 60
Salerno, Gino, 149
San Jose, 47
Sanders, Barry, 8
Santa Fe Railroad, 24, 125
Scott, Brady, 55
Scottish Rite Temple, 146, 147
Scurfield, Marcia K., 116
Sedgwick County, 112, 129
Sedgwick County Courthouse, 113, 142
Sedgwick County Park, 148, 149
Senator Long, 25
Sewing History Museum, 112, 113
Shadowland Dance Hall, 60
Sheldon Coleman Tennis Complex, 34
Sherman, Denise, 69
Sidepockets, 154, 155
Snow White, 110
Society of Friends, 92
Solar Calendar, 32, 33
Soldiers & Sailors Monument, 142, 143
South Lawrence Street Bridge, 89
Southwestern Railroad, 10
Spanish-American War, 120, 121
Spice Merchant, The, 164, 165
Spirit Hunters Paranormal Society, 84
Stanley, Governor W. E., 120
Station 8 BBQ, 118, 119, 135
Statue of Liberty, 16, 50, 51
Stearman, Lloyd, 84, 85, 102
Stearman Model 4D, 84
SteelCraft, 166
Sterling College, 134
Stickwork, 90
Stockton, Katrina, 112
Suber, Baxter "Slim", 55
Sunflower State, 66, 67
Tarutu, 96
TempleLive, 146, 147
Together Wichita, 108
Towanda, 10
Towne East Square, 144
Trailblazers Hall of Fame, 69
Troll, 4, 5

**183**

Tulsa, 166
Tunnel of Trees, 22, 23
Twin Beech, 18
*Two Steers*, 49
Ulrich Museum of Art, 98, 99
Unified School District 259, 29
Union Station Plaza, 25
United States Constitution, 80–81
United States Army, 110
United States Navy, 48
USS *Monitor*, 97
Viquesney, E. M., 142
W. A. Jones Building, 150
Wagonmasters' Chili Cook-off, 162, 163
Walsh, Joe, 60
Wasabi Hinkaku, 116
WaterWalk Wichita, 87
Waverly, 20
*Weekly Eagle*, the, 46, 47
Western Lithograph, 12
*Western Methodist*, 72
Wheatshockers, 135
Whitaker, J. P., 50
Wichita Art Museum, 42, 43
Wichita Association of Retired School Personnel, 29
Wichita Bar Association, 50
Wichita Baseball Museum, 156, 157
*Wichita Beacon*, the, 57, 134
Wichita Boathouse, 152, 153
Wichita Community Foundation, 76, 116
*Wichita Daily Beacon*, the, 164
*Wichita Eagle*, the, 20, 24, 64, 74, 86, 92, 144
Wichita Festival Inc., 162
Wichita Fire Department, 118
Wichita Force, 134
Wichita Hospital, 14
Wichita Indians, 8, 10, 56
Wichita Model Train Show, 31
*Wichita Reader*, The, 80
Wichita River Festival, 162, 163
Wichita Rotary Club, 63
Wichita Savings Bank, 57
Wichita State University, 21, 34, 35, 49, 70, 98, 104, 124, 128, 129, 132, 134, 158, 160
Wichita Toy Train Club & Museum, 30
Wichita Veterans Memorial Park, 4
Wichita Wagonmasters, 162
Wichita Wind Surge, 156, 157
Wichita-Sedgwick County Historical Museum, 46, 47, 61, 74, 75, 140, 141, 165
Wichitennial, 12
Wild West, 14, 15, 170
Williams, Kent, 124
Williams, Marilyn, 109
*Window in Time*, 45
Windwagon, 162, 163
Windwagon Smith, 162, 163
Women of Aviation, 20, 21
Wonderland Park, 6, 7
Woodard, Lynette, 8
Woodman, W. C., 65
World War I, 62
World War II, 18, 48, 58, 63, 67, 110, 111
Wright, Frank Lloyd, 70
Wright, Olgivanna, 71
Wurlitzer, 82
WuShock Drive, 34, 99
YMCA, 146, 165
Yard, The, 18, 19
Yellow Brick Road, The, 38, 136
Yucca Company, The, 164
Zerbe Family Sleeping Troll Hill, 5